LAW
ENFORCEMENT
AGENCIES

BORDER
PATROL

LAW ENFORCEMENT AGENCIES

Bomb Squad

Border Patrol

Federal Bureau of Investigation

The Secret Service

SWAT Teams

The Texas Rangers

LAW
ENFORCEMENT
AGENCIES

BORDER PATROL

William Weir

CHELSEA HOUSE
PUBLISHERS
An imprint of Infobase Publishing

BORDER PATROL

Chelsea House
An imprint of Infobase Publishing
132 West 31st Street
New York NY 10001

Library of Congress Cataloging-in-Publication Data

Weir, William.
Border patrol / William Weir. — 1st ed.
p. cm. — (Law enforcement agencies)
Includes bibliographical references and index.
ISBN-13: 978-1-60413-635-7 (hardcover : alk. paper)
ISBN-10: 1-60413-635-9 (hardcover : alk. paper) 1. Border patrols—United States—
Juvenile literature. 2. U.S. Customs and Border Protection—Juvenile literature. I. Title.
JV6483.W43 2010
363.28'50973—dc22   2010030051

Chelsea House books are available at special discounts when purchased
in bulk quantities for businesses, associations, institutions,
or sales promotions. Please call our Special Sales Department
in New York at (212) 967-8800 or (800) 322-8755.

You can find Chelsea House on the World Wide Web at http://www.chelseahouse.com

Text design and composition by Erika K. Arroyo
Cover design by Keith Trego
Cover printed by Bang Printing, Brainerd, Minn.
Book printed and bound by Bang Printing, Brainerd, MN
Date printed: November 2010

Printed in the United States of America

10 9 8 7 6 5 4 3 2 1

This book is printed on acid-free paper.

All links and Web addresses were checked and verified to be correct
at the time of publication. Because of the dynamic nature of the Web,
some addresses and links may have changed since publication and may no longer be valid.

Contents

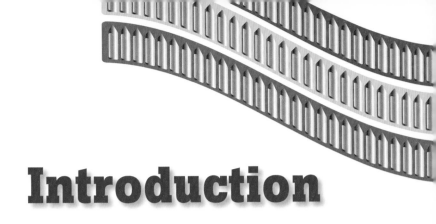

Introduction

In 2009 the U.S. Border Patrol celebrated its 85th birthday, but it is actually older than that. It was founded in 1924, but it had been preceded by the Mounted Watchmen created in 1904 by Theodore Roosevelt. The Watchmen's principal duty was to intercept Chinese crossing the southern border of the United States. The government gave them badges and sometimes revolvers, but no uniforms. They wore civilian clothes and provided their own horses and saddles.

To say that the Watchmen operated on a shoestring would be a gross exaggeration. It was more like a broken shoestring without a tip. The force at its largest fielded 75 men, each of whom made $24 a month. It was charged with patrolling the border with Mexico from San Diego, California, on the Pacific Coast, to Brownsville, Texas, on the Gulf Coast, a distance of about 2,000 miles. But, as the Border Patrol official history admits, "Their efforts were irregular and undertaken only when resources permitted."[1]

In 1915 Congress authorized a new group, known as the Mounted Guards or Mounted Inspectors, which included most of the former Mounted Watchmen. The number of guards increased, but they still furnished their own clothes, horses, and saddles. Now, though, they got an allowance for feed for the horses and a salary of $1,680 a year.

There was no formal training. The men recruited were former police officers who were familiar with both horses and guns. Alumni of the Texas Rangers were a substantial part of the force. In 1915 the Mexican border was a dangerous place. The Mexican Revolution against Porfirio Diaz had begun in 1910 and reached its height when the Mounted Guards were first deployed. But the Mexican border is a long way from most of the populated parts of the United States. The Guards' exploits and perils were largely unknown to their fellow citizens. This beneath-the-radar status continued even during the truly dangerous days of Prohibition and the Great Depression, when the Border Patrol engaged in 20 times more gunfights than the Federal Bureau of Investigation (FBI).[2]

During the Great Depression, illegal aliens, whether Asian or Latino, were not much of a problem. They came to America to find jobs, and there were no jobs available. The lack of jobs discouraged immigrants. There was another lack in the United States that did, however, cause problems—the lack of alcohol. This dearth offered a great opportunity for the criminal element both here and abroad. In Chicago, for example, a talented burglar named Dion O'Bannion found that bootlegging was an easier way to make money than theft. He enlisted other crooks, including George "Bugs" Moran, who previously specialized in stealing dray horses and holding them for ransom. O'Bannion and Moran were soon fighting for turf with Johnny Torrio, who managed a string

Black cloth covers the badge of a United States Border Patrol agent in the wake of the death of a fellow agent. *(AP Photo/Lenny Ignelzi)*

of bordellos in New York, and his "muscle," Al Capone. Foreign criminals, too, jumped on the gravy, or rather, booze train. Mexican cattle rustlers and smugglers, who had previously sneaked Chinese across the border, now escorted mule trains carrying liquor. With the anarchy that accompanied the Mexican Revolution, it was easy to organize smuggling expeditions.

In the United States the Depression motivated gunmen like John Dillinger and Clyde Barrow to rob banks; Prohibition inspired crooks like Dutch Schultz and Frank Costello to deal in illegal alcohol. There was plenty of violent crime, but there was more of it in Mexico. The Revolution bred violent men, and some of the revolutionaries, like Pancho Villa, had been bandits in civilian life. Life along "the Line," as the border was sometimes called, became very dangerous, especially for those charged with stopping smuggling. The Border Patrolmen occasionally used cars (most of them jalopies) at this time, but did most of their patrolling in the saddle. After World War I the government issued revolvers—.45 caliber M1917 army surplus weapons. Most patrolmen, though—an unusually gun-savvy crew—preferred their own handguns. They also bought semiautomatic rifles and repeating shotguns because they needed more firepower.

Following the Depression, the Border Patrol became more professional. A training academy was established and the Patrol got new equipment like airplanes, autogiros (a forerunner of the helicopter), and jeeps. The government issued new guns, more appropriate to the work the Border Patrolmen had to do. As always, illegal immigration was a problem for the Patrol, and during World War II, the federal government established the Bracero Program, to bring Mexican guest workers into the country to relieve the manpower shortage, which complicated securing the border.

Illegal immigration increased after the war and the immigrants, defenseless and afraid to contact American police, attracted bandits from Mexico, who crossed the border to rob them. Another problem was the number of illegal immigrants who took wilderness routes into the country and died in the desert or mountains.

Drug smuggling became an increasing problem during this time as well. The Border Patrol not only attacked it on the border, it also sent its agents out of the country to help train foreign drug police.

The Border Patrol has emphasized the Mexican border during most of its existence, but it is also responsible for the security of American islands in the Caribbean and the Canadian border. In the age of terrorism, it has been beefing up these other areas, especially the Canadian border, using everything from Bureau of Land Management mustangs to remote control television cameras and unmanned drone aircraft. But it now seems that the biggest problem in the future is going to be the vicious drug cartels in Mexico, which are increasing their reach into the United States.

Unfortunately the work of the Border Patrol is not well known to the average American. Operating quietly has become a Border Patrol tradition.

As Senior Patrol Agent Alex Pacheco put it, "Historically the patrol has voluntarily remained in the shadows, gladly allowing other agencies to earn credit for our greatest victories. While the FBI and DEA (Drug Enforcement Agency) fight for camera time, BORTAC, the Border Patrol's national tactical team, covertly travels around the world, breaking up riots, infiltrating smuggling organizations, and training foreign drug police."[3]

To the average American today, the Border Patrol is an organization that spends all its time tracking down illegal aliens and deporting them, even when it means breaking up families. Its agents do apprehend illegal aliens—mostly at the border—but as Pacheco and his co-author Erich Krauss point out, the patrolmen don't make the law, they just enforce it.[4] The Border Patrol also rescues aliens abandoned in the desert and dying of thirst. And they have protected the immigrants by arresting bandits who prey on the immigrants, even when that meant letting the immigrants go. They have also arrested suspected terrorists, although there have been very few of them (and most terrorists arrested came from Canada rather than Mexico). But their most dangerous job has been coping with smugglers, who sometimes appear to have been escorted by the Mexican military. There were more than 100 crossings of the border by Mexican troops prior to the spring of 2002, according to Pacheco and Krauss.[5]

Those hard-boiled gunslingers of the Depression-era would never have dreamed that the border guards of today would have such things as night-vision glasses, fully automatic rifles, electronic alarms installed along the border, helicopters, airplanes, and even unmanned Predator drones more modern than some of those now in use in Afghanistan and Iraq.

The history of the United States Border Patrol is a rags-to-riches saga that few other law enforcement agencies can match.

Chapter 1, "Development of the Border Patrol," outlines how the service grew from 75 patrolmen who supplied their own horses and guns to thousands of agents with airplanes, helicopters, remote controlled drones, and the highest of high-tech equipment.

Chapter 2, "How the Service Began," covers the handful of Mounted Watchmen that began patrolling the border with Mexico in 1904.

Chapter 3, "Prohibition and Gunfighting," chronicles the advent of Prohibition and the Border Patrol's response to the rapid rise in liquor smuggling.

Chapter 4, "New Professionalism," deals with tactical and technological improvements in the Border Patrol, including its first academy, cars equipped with radios, airplanes, autogiros, and new weapons.

Chapter 5, "Smuggling People," covers the people-smuggling brought on by the end of the "Bracero" program, which welcomed Mexican farm laborers. More and more people tried to cross the border illegally, and guiding them became a criminal specialty in Mexico.

Chapter 6, "The Bandit Teams," discusses the Mexican thugs that crossed the border to rob and terrorize would-be immigrants, and the "bandit teams" formed by the Border Patrol and San Diego police to arrest these criminals.

Chapter 7, "BORSTAR and BORTAC," deals with the Border Patrol's two elite corps: BORSTAR, which rescues people trapped in the desert or the mountains, and BORTAC, which trains foreign police in antinarcotics operations.

Chapter 8, "The North Country and 9/11," describes the increased attention given to the Canadian border as a result of the September 11, 2001, terrorist attacks.

Chapter 9, "The Cartels," recounts the Border Patrol's ongoing battle against Mexican drug cartels, which have become a serious threat and have extended their reach as far as Alaska.

Development of the Border Patrol

The desert hills of eastern San Diego were very dark on this night in 1978. What light there was came from a sliver of moon and the stars as well as the glow of city lights on clouds to the west. Six men in dirty, ragged clothes sat on the ground. They looked strangely bulky, as if they were wearing two or three sets of clothing. That's because they were; Mexicans crossing the border illegally didn't carry suitcases. They heard footsteps and the rustle of weeds along the trail leading from Mexico. Soon, they were able to make out three men approaching them.

"What are you doing here?" the first man asked in Spanish.

"Waiting for our guide," one of the seated men answered in Spanish.

"He may not show up," the first man said. "The border's a danger-ous place, even for an experienced old coyote. I don't know how much experience your coyote has. We have plenty of experience. You'd better come with us."

"I don't think so," the seated man said. "We paid him already."

The first man reached down with his left hand, grabbed the seated man by the collar, jerked him upright, and pulled a knife on him. The other two standing men drew pistols.

Suddenly, the ground seemed to explode. All of the seated men were firing pistols. A couple of men were firing with a gun in each hand.

All three of the strangers went down. Two were dead. One was still alive—barely.[1]

The men who had been sitting on the ground were not illegal immigrants—*pollos* ("chickens" in Mexican slang). They were American police officers: three Border Patrol agents and three San Diego policemen. The three men who approached them were not guides or *coyotes*, as they called themselves. They were bandits who came up from Mexico to rob illegal immigrants on the American side of the border. It was a pretty safe racket. The pollos had no weapons as guns were practically impossible for an honest citizen of Mexico to obtain. The immigrants would not try to contact American police for fear that they'd be jailed or at least deported.

The bandits frequently killed the people they robbed, and they routinely raped any women they found out in the desert. The man with the knife appeared to be preparing a typical bandit operation—cut up one of the *pollos* to intimidate the others.

In 1976 the bandit situation had gotten so bad that the San Diego police and Border Patrol organized anti-bandit teams and finally drove the bandits back across the border. The teams were disbanded in 1978, and the bandits came back.

Beginning in 1924 with 450 officers, the Border Patrol now has more than 20,000 agents, making it one of the fastest-growing police agencies in the country. The service has doubled since 2001.Those 20,000 agents, though, are hardly too many for its task—guarding about 10,000 miles of U.S. borders.

Its tasks have grown almost as much as its personnel, but the average American, if he or she thinks about the Border Patrol at all, may think its agents are pleasant people with an undemanding job, and that their only duty is to ask if you are an American citizen when you return from a trip to Mexico or Canada. To some, though, they are nasty types who hunt down illegal aliens and send them back where they came from, even if it means breaking up families. Both images are equally false.

The patrol has a different public image than other law enforcement groups—federal, state, and local. It does not have the pizzazz of the Federal Bureau of Investigation (FBI) or the Drug Enforcement Administration (DEA) or even the Bureau of Alcohol, Tobacco, Firearms and Explosives (ATF). The U.S. Marshals retain the phony glamour of Wyatt Earp (who never was a marshal—one of Wyatt's many lies). Local Special Weapons and Tactics, or SWAT, teams are credited with extraordinary heroism, but no other agency except the military has had as many desperate gunfights as the Border Patrol. Nobody thinks of Border Patrol agents rappelling from helicopters, confronting foreign troops, or participating in secret missions in foreign countries, but they do all of this.

The Federal Bureau of Investigation and the Secret Service have had television series made about their activities. So have the Texas Rangers and big city police departments like Miami, Los Angeles, and New York. Not the Border Patrol, though.

The Border Patrol's basic job is to keep people and goods not allowed in the country out of it. That, however, may involve everything from following almost invisible tracks in the desert to locating cocaine laboratories in the Bolivian jungle. Border Patrol agents might fly helicopters to rescue lost souls stranded on mountaintops or engage in firefights with drug smugglers in crowded border towns. They might "fly" pilotless drones over the Mexican border, ride Bureau of Land Management mustangs through the mountains on the Canadian border, monitor electronic sensors on land borders, or even patrol coastal waters in the Caribbean and the Gulf of Mexico.

The original, traditional job of the Border Patrol has been to keep undocumented aliens out of the United States. That was the main emphasis of the Mounted Watchmen and the Mounted Guards before the birth of the Border Patrol. Xenophobia (fear of aliens) was, in fact, what led to the creation of the Border Patrol. Waves of xenophobia have been a recurring phenomenon throughout U.S. history, from the Chinese before the turn of the 20th century, to Mexicans after World Wars I and II, to Latinos in general today. Currently fear of aliens and fear of terrorists, as well as the criminal activities of Mexican drug gangs, fuels the Border Patrol's unprecedented expansion.

More exciting and more dangerous than stopping undocumented aliens has been the task of keeping out first alcohol and then drugs. After the terrorist attacks of September 11, 2001, keeping out terrorists and their weapons was added—emphatically—to those tasks. To all those other duties has recently been added keeping order in border towns and putting down riots in detention camps, such as those created following the 1980 Mariel boatlift, a mass exodus of Cubans from Cuba to the United States.

The original Border Patrolmen got feed for their horses, badges, and revolvers (which many of them disdained) from the government. Four years later, they got uniforms. In the 1930s they got an academy, airplanes, and autogiros. Along the way, the Patrol organized itself into districts and a hierarchy of officers. After World War II, it got jeeps and nearly useless radios. In the last 20 years, though, the Border Patrol has gotten new weapons, new radios, new vehicles, new aircraft, remote control television cameras, vibration sensors, night vision glasses, and other gadgets. Further, these are no longer army

A dual-engine United States Border Patrol boat surveys the Rio Grande and Texas's border with Mexico. (*Bob Daemmrich/Corbis*)

THE AUTOGIRO

At first glance, it looks like a helicopter. A helicopter, however, doesn't have a propeller in the front, as the autogiro does. Millions of people today have never seen one; millions have never even heard of one. It was invented in the early 1920s by Spanish engineer Juan de la Cierva, who made his first flight on January 9, 1923. Inventors for decades had been trying to produce a workable helicopter. Cierva's vehicle was a step in that direction, but it wasn't a helicopter. In its day, in the 1930s, however, it was considered a kind of miracle aircraft. It could take off in a very short space. Newsreel film showed one taking off from the roof of the 30th Street Post Office in Philadelphia.

Unlike a helicopter, the autogiro could not take off straight up, nor could it land the same way. There was no power to its rotors; they rotated when the aircraft moved forward and provided far more "lift" than fixed wings. The pilot could control the amount of lift by varying the pitch of the rotors. Some autogiros had a clutch that could transfer power from the engine to the rotors for a brief period, giving this antique whirly bird a kind of bounce on takeoff.

Although it was not a true helicopter, the autogiro could take off and land in terrain that would be impossible for fixed-wing aircraft. That made it a most useful vehicle for the Border Patrol.

surplus. In some cases, this new equipment is more modern than the army's equipment.

Since 2003, the Border Patrol has been part of the Department of Homeland Security. Like every other group in that department, its principal job is protecting the country from enemy terrorists. It has caught some terrorists like the Millennium Bomber, Ahmed Ressam, an Algerian who in December 1999 tried to smuggle explosives into the

The Border Patrol utilized autogiros in the 1930s because they could take off and land in areas inaccessible to other aircraft available at the time. *(Science Faction/Corbis)*

United States from Canada to bomb Los Angeles International Airport. But terrorists are in short supply compared to drug smugglers, and the representatives of the Mexican cartels are fully as vicious as any terrorists. They are the most dangerous people on the border, and they are extending their operations into the United States, to places as far north as Alaska.

How the Service Began

In 1906, in Brownsville, Texas, a border town at the southern tip of Texas, a pair of soldiers, James Newton and Frank Lipscomb, were walking on the sidewalk. Several women were standing on the sidewalk ahead of them. As the soldiers started to pass them, a customs agent named Tate dashed across the street, pulled out a revolver, and hit Newton on the head with it. He then pointed the gun at the soldier's head and would have shot him if Lipscomb and other bystanders had not pulled him away. Tate claimed the soldier had "jostled" the women.

A short time later, a soldier named Reed was crossing the bridge connecting Brownsville with Matamoros, Mexico, when a customs agent suddenly grabbed him and threw him into the Rio Grande.

What had Reed done?

He, like Newton and Lipscomb, had been born black.

At the time of this incident, the population of Brownsville was largely of Mexican descent, but all power was in the hands of "Anglos," which is what Mexicans called anybody who had no Hispanic origin. In Brownsville, at this time, the Anglo culture was that of the racist Deep South.

In 1906 the all-black 25th Infantry Regiment was sent to Fort Brown, located inside the city of Brownsville. Senator C.A. Culberson of Texas wrote to William Howard Taft, the secretary of war, protesting the move of black soldiers into Brownsville. Taft refused to change the order. Hostility to the soldiers grew among Brownsville's white-Anglo population. In no group was there more hostility than among the border guards.

Incidents like these multiplied, and the mood of the Anglo population of Brownsville grew so ugly that the commanding officer of the fort canceled all passes. Around midnight that same day, there was a burst of gunfire that lasted about 10 minutes. Thinking the fort was under attack, the sergeant of the guard ordered the bugler to sound the call to arms. All of the soldiers, except a few that were in the hospital, fell in. The firing ended, however, as the soldiers were issued weapons.

The next day, Brownsville authorities complained that a group of black soldiers—the number varied from nine to 30, according to the accounts of various Brownsville citizens—had climbed the fort's wall and rampaged through the town. A police lieutenant had been shot and wounded and a bartender killed. The police showed the fort commander some 70 .30-06 cartridge shells that fit the new Model 1903 Springfield rifle, a weapon used by the army but unavailable to civilians.

The mayor of Brownsville sent a telegram to President Theodore Roosevelt demanding that the black soldiers be moved out of Brownsville. Roosevelt ordered an investigation. All of the soldiers denied doing any shooting, and none of them was allowed to cross-examine the accusers. The officer in charge of the investigation recommended that all of the soldiers (except those in the hospital) be discharged without honor. This is not the same as a dishonorable discharge, which can only be ordered by a court martial, but someone discharged in this way is barred for life from any military or other federal employment.

Roosevelt agreed to the discharges, although the investigators ignored a number of inconvenient facts:

1. When the call to arms sounded, all of the soldiers, except those in the hospital, fell in. None of them were shooting outside.
2. If any of the soldiers had been outside, they had nothing to shoot with, at least not government rifles. The rifles were distributed after the call to arms.
3. All witnesses agreed that they heard about 200 shots, but only 70 shells were found.

4. Most of the shells found in Brownsville had not been fired in the rifles in Fort Brown. The shells had been shipped to Fort Brown from other army posts for reloading, and they had been kept in open containers available to anyone who walked through the fort.

5. There were no streetlights in Brownsville. At midnight it would have been impossible to know if someone in the street were white or black, a soldier or a civilian.

Roosevelt had gained the reputation of being racially unbiased because he had entertained Booker T. Washington with dinner at the White House. But he lied about the conduct of black troops in Cuba, although they saved his Rough Riders at Las Guasimas and led the way in the Battle of San Juan Hill.[1] He wasn't about to buck public opinion in this case. In 1972 President Richard Nixon changed the discharges without honor to honorable discharges. By that time, only one of the soldiers was still alive.

Who really did the shooting remains a mystery, but the federal officers, who had shown such violence and hostility to the black soldiers, are hardly above suspicion.[2]

These customs agents were not Border Patrolmen. The Border Patrol would not be founded for another nine years, but there was a connection. Racism was the obvious cause of the Brownsville incident. The racism that led to the creation of the Border Patrol was directed against the Chinese, who began coming to the West Coast soon after the Gold Rush (1850s to 1880s). The U.S. occupation of California greatly increased trans-Pacific trade, and inhabitants of China saw economic opportunities. So did the California railroad magnates, who knew the Chinese would work for less than Americans or European immigrants. But after the railroads were built, Chinese were accused of taking American jobs (and, among the most virulent anti-Chinese citizens, of running opium dens and seducing American women).

In 1882 a law was passed banning Chinese from entering the United States. It was renewed repeatedly and in 1902 it was finally made indefinite. It was not repealed until 1943, when China was an ally in World War II.

Unable to land in the United States, the Chinese went to Mexico. They then took the Mexican Central Railroad to Ciudad Juárez and entered the United States at El Paso. "Even though they were often treated on a subhuman level once they reached American soil—utilized when needed, discarded when not—they continued to pour in by the thousands," Krauss and Pacheco write.[3] In 1904, to cope with the flood of banned Chinese, the federal government created a new force, the Mounted Watchmen, to patrol the open country when they weren't needed at the entry ports. For many Watchmen, however, that was not often. The Mounted Watchmen force was truly the red-headed stepchild of federal law enforcement. It never included more than 75 officers, who furnished their own clothes, horses, and saddles. They made $24 a month to support themselves and their horses, and they often furnished their own weapons.

These law enforcers were supposed to be concerned exclusively with Chinese border crossers. The Chinese immigrants were mostly nonviolent, and their guides, the spiritual ancestors of today's "coyotes," would sooner abandon their charges in the desert than shoot it out with American lawmen. Nevertheless, the small Watchman force was supposed to patrol the entire land boundary between the United States and Mexico, so a Watchman was almost sure to be outnumbered by any group of illegal immigrants he encountered.

Because of this, the government recruited the toughest gunfighters they could find. One of these was a former Texas Ranger named Jeff Davis Milton. Milton had joined the Rangers in 1880. To become a Ranger, Milton had to demonstrate his ability with a revolver. The Rangers, hardened gunfighters all, found his expertise breathtaking. Milton served only four years in the Texas Rangers, though. He left in disgust after he was charged with and acquitted of murder when he killed a popular rancher in self-defense.

Milton moved to Arizona, where he worked as a deputy sheriff and a cattle detective. In that state, he worked for John Slaughter, sheriff of Cochise County and one of the West's greatest gunmen, and partnered with another great gunman, George Scarborough. Western historian Eugene Cunningham, one of the country's leading experts on the gunmen of the Old West, said, "Milton is one of the really great old-time officers and as a gun expert need touch his hat to very, very few!"[4]

At one time, Jeff Milton was guarding a safe full of gold in a railroad car when the gang of Burt Alvord, a lawman turned bandit, tried to rob the train. One of the gang shot Milton in the left arm. The ex-Ranger grabbed his shotgun with his right hand and killed two of the robbers. Then he closed the car door, put the key to the safe inside the safe, locked the safe, and passed out. Alvord and his men got into the railroad car while Milton lay unconscious but they couldn't open the safe. They left, frustrated.

Milton later moved to El Paso, Texas, and became a customs inspector. Chasing smugglers took him all through the deserts of New Mexico and Arizona in the late 1880s, where, among other things, he learned from the Papago Indians how to survive in the desert. After the Customs Service was temporarily disbanded in 1889, he became police chief of El Paso.

As police chief, Milton was occasionally associated with John Wesley Hardin, perhaps the baddest bad man in the West. Hardin, who had killed 40 men in the course of his activities, became a lawyer after his release from prison. Milton helped Hardin when the lawyer was attempting to have two rustlers extradited from Mexico. They did not always see eye to eye. At one time, Cunningham says, witnesses saw Milton slap Hardin's face, an act most men would have considered suicidal.[5]

Congress continued to pass laws restricting immigration, and immigrants continued to cross the border. Chinese still made up the bulk of the illegal immigrants. In 1904, when the Mounted Watchmen was organized, President Theodore Roosevelt appointed Jeff Milton to the position of "Mounted Chinese Inspector." Supervision of the far-flung Watchmen was almost nonexistent. Milton rode far and wide, tracking illegal aliens. He discovered "Chinese farms," places where illegal aliens waited while their guides arranged to bring them to promised jobs.

In 1915 the Mounted Watchmen were replaced by a new force, the Mounted Guards. The Guards were a larger outfit than the Watchmen. The Guards included veterans of the Watchmen force, ex-lawmen, and former Railroad Mail clerks, who sorted letters on moving trains and carried guns to discourage train robbers. The Colt firearms company

THE SPRINGFIELD RIFLE

Modern rifle shooters who read about the Brownsville affair may be puzzled by the fact that shells for the Springfield rifle cartridge could have been fired only in an army rifle. Today, the .30-06 Springfield cartridge is the most common centerfire rifle cartridge in the United States and one of the most common in the world.

In 1906, though, there was little civilian demand for bolt-action rifles. American hunters preferred lever actions, like the Winchesters seen in many cowboy movies. The army adopted its first general-issue bolt action, the Krag–Jorgensen, in 1892 because it was easier to use from a prone position than a lever action. In the Spanish-American War of 1898, the Krag proved to be inferior to the Spanish Mauser. After the war, the United States adopted a modified Mauser, the Springfield 1903. It issued a few Springfields when the Germans introduced a new type of cartridge with a "spitzer" (pointed) bullet. The United States developed its own spitzer cartridge and recalled the new Springfields to rechamber them in 1906. That is why the M1903 Springfield rifle shoots the .30-06 cartridge.

In 1906 there were no civilian rifles to handle the .30-06 cartridge. Demand for such weapons increased after World War I, when large numbers of Americans had to learn to use bolt-action rifles.

introduced its "Bankers Special" revolver for the Railroad Mail Service. The Mounted Guards were better paid than the Watchmen: The annual salary was $1,680, and they were given oats for their horses. Like the Watchmen, their primary duty was to stem the flow of illegal immigrants, chiefly Chinese, into the country. They also tried to stop smuggling, although that was not yet a major problem.

When the Watchmen were formed, however, Mexico was having serious troubles, which were soon to spread across the border. The Watchmen, like the Mounted Guards, were overwhelmed.

CIVILIANS IN COLUMBUS

"I was awakened about four A.M. by the sound of shots," said rancher Buck Chadborn, who was also a deputy sheriff and cattle inspector.[6] Jack Thomas, another deputy sheriff and a cowboy on Chadborn's ranch, was staying at the house. At first the lawmen thought the shooting was just some cowboys celebrating. Nevertheless, they hid their wives and children in a cyclone cellar and rode into town.

"By the time we got to town, there were several buildings burning," Chadborn recalled. "In the light from the fire, we could see a milling mob of Mexicans wearing the big sombreros and crossed gun belts of Pancho Villa's followers. There were bands of them, shooting and yelling 'Viva Villa!' and 'Viva Mexico!' The Commercial Hotel was blazing. I remember a couple of Customs men, Jolly Garner [the nephew of John Nance Garner, the vice president in Franklin D. Roosevelt's first term] and Ben Aguirre, saving a woman on the second floor of the hotel. They got her out and down by lowering her with sheets tied together. The hotel burned clear to the ground."[7]

Before Chadborn and Thomas arrived, Villista troops had entered the hotel. They pulled one guest, William Walton, away from his wife and shot him on the stairs. They took two other men, Dr. H.M. Hart and Charles Miller, into the street and robbed them. Then they killed them. Steven Burchfield was in his room when he heard the commotion. He opened the door and told the attackers in fluent Spanish that he'd give them all his money. He threw bills and coins on the hall floor, slammed the door and left by the fire escape.

Chadborn and Taylor found another friend of Chadborn's, Dick Rodriguez. Together, they started organizing the men of the town to fight back. In Columbus, almost every man had a gun of some sort, and the Villistas were unable to hold the town.[8]

REVOLUTION ACROSS THE BORDER

A little after midnight on March 9, 1916, a large group of men crossed the Mexico–U.S. border. They were mounted and they wore wide-brimmed sombreros on their heads and cartridge belts crisscrossed over their chests. They rode a short distance toward the town of Columbus, New Mexico. Then the leaders dismounted and began leading their horses so their passage would be quieter. The men split into two parties. One party crept into the town of Columbus. There were no streetlights and most of the oil lamps in the houses had been blown out hours ago. The other party entered the grounds of Camp Furlong, a cavalry base. Suddenly gunfire broke out.

There were screams of "Mata a los gringos!" ("Kill the gringos!") Newspapers in the United States reported a massacre of Americans by Mexican revolutionists, followers of Pancho Villa, a former bandit. What happened at Columbus was quite different from a "massacre." The soldiers at Camp Furlong had rallied and mowed down the raid-

U.S. militia troops stand behind captured raiders from Pancho Villa's band who invaded Columbus, New Mexico, in March 1916. *(Bettmann/Corbis)*

ers. Then a troop of cavalry had chased Villa's men far across the border.

What the Columbus incident did was emphasize how dangerous the southern U.S. border had become. The Mexican Revolution had begun in 1910 to overthrow Porfirio Diaz, a would-be president-for-life. The revolutionary armies then fought each other in a struggle for supremacy. The revolution theoretically ended in 1920, but fighting went on until the mid-1930s, during the administration of President Lazaro Cardenas. During most of the revolution, Pancho Villa had been a friend of the United States. He bought most of his weapons and supplies in this country and took refuge in El Paso, Texas, when one of his rivals, Victoriano Huerta, became president and was hunting him. He later returned and joined other revolutionaries in overthrowing Huerta. Villa welcomed American correspondents, and they wrote glowing reports about his activities. He was the average American's favorite revolutionist. He was not a favorite of President Woodrow Wilson, though.

American troops march into Mexico in pursuit of Pancho Villa and his followers, crossing territory south of Columbus, New Mexico, in 1916. *(Bettmann/Corbis)*

When Wilson threw his support to another of Villa's rivals, Venustiano Carranza, Villa felt betrayed, and he attacked Columbus.

The Villa raid led to a punitive expedition into Mexico by the U.S. Army. It failed to capture Villa, and the border remained a dangerous place for years.

The Border Patrol was created in 1924 in a time and place of peril. The revolution had greatly unsettled all Mexican civil society. Thousands of men now believed that they carried the law in their holsters. And events in the United States had greatly increased the possibilities of making a dishonest dollar.

The Mexican Revolution itself had much less to do with the Border Patrol than with the U.S. Military. The U.S. Navy occupied the Mexican port of Veracruz in 1914 and stayed until 1917.

The revolution's effect on the Border Patrol was indirect. The war in Mexico fostered the development of a lot of violent and lawless men who found robbery and smuggling more congenial than poorly paid labor on farms and ranches.

Prohibition and Gunfighting

Through the window of their car, the three-man Border Patrol team saw some suspicious-looking men on Cordova Island, a section of El Paso, Texas, that at this time (the late 1920s) was no longer an island, the Rio Grande having changed its channel. The Border Patrolmen were well armed. In addition to their revolvers, two had .351 caliber semiautomatic rifles and the third, Charles Askins—who later became a pistol champion, army colonel, and writer—had a 12-gauge pump shotgun. The men on Cordova Island looked like the vanguard of a liquor-smuggling expedition.

The patrolmen stopped their car and crept toward the "island" along back streets. It turned out that the smugglers were in the process of setting up an ambush for lawmen. Unaware that the patrolmen had left their car, six of the smugglers were moving into position. There was a full moon and the Border Patrol agents could see the crooks easily. Somebody fired a shot, and then the air filled with flying lead. Askins fired at a big man carrying a shotgun. When the big man fell, he fired at another *pistolero*. This man, the border guards later learned, had already been hit squarely in the chest with a .351 rifle slug that shredded his heart. He didn't fall, though. He continued firing. He was using a very old, single-action .44 caliber Smith & Wesson Russian model revolver. Askins fired two loads of buckshot into him, and the man still thumbed back the hammer of his museum-piece revolver as he slid slowly to the ground and died.

"I found a single ten dollar bill in his watch pocket after we got him to the coroner," Askins wrote. "His pay was roughly three times that of the average gunman and certainly he was worth three times the ordinary in sheer guts alone."[1]

After World War I, illegal immigration from Mexico had ceased to be a problem for the United States. During World War I, the United States experienced a shortage of young men—the sort of shortage it had not experienced since the Civil War. Farms and factories which had depended on unskilled labor were in trouble. To meet the shortage, Congress dropped the restrictions it had imposed on immigrants, such as literacy, and employers sent recruiters into Mexico. Mexican immigration, which had been small compared with immigration from Europe, increased rapidly. Bandit raids, although still a problem, were diminishing as the Mexican Revolution wound down.

Then a new law in the United States made immigration a distinctly minor problem for the gatekeepers on America's frontiers. At midnight, January 16, 1920, it became illegal to manufacture, sell, or import alcoholic beverages to the United States. Alcohol, unlike aliens, did not get thirsty, hungry, or tired. It did not run away or die in the desert. It did not take up much space, and smuggling it was more profitable and less complicated than smuggling aliens. Finding buyers for illegal liquor was easier than finding employers for illegal aliens. People who had been smuggling aliens switched to smuggling booze. Former revolutionary soldiers joined them. The Mounted Guards were overrun.

Once again, the U.S. government created a new body of gatekeepers. On May 28, 1924, the U.S. Border Patrol was born. It was to secure the land borders between inspection stations. In 1925 its jurisdiction was extended to include the seacoasts. Its strength was set at 450 inspectors, once again recruited largely from state and local police officers and the gun-toting Railroad Mail clerks. The Border Patrol was part of the Immigration Service, later named the Immigration and Naturalization Service (INS), which, in turn, was part of the Labor Department. The INS later moved to the Department of Justice. Theoretically, the Border Patrol's primary mission was to prevent illegal immigration. Actually, it was more concerned with preventing the importation of illegal alcohol.

That is why, at first, the majority of inspectors went to the Canadian border, where Canadian bootleggers had close ties with American gangsters like the Purple Gang in Detroit, Al Capone and Dion O'Bannion in Chicago, and Dutch Schultz and assorted Mafiosi in New York.

More liquor may have crossed the Canadian border, but more blood was spilled along the Mexican border. The Border Patrol began shifting its strength to the southern border. The revolution had left Mexico with a surplus of gunmen who were willing to work for very little. The usual organization of a smuggling expedition was for the toughest and most experienced gunslingers to lead the caravan, with newcomers or less talented gunners bringing up the rear. In the middle was the booze, carried by horses, burros, mules, or human mules. The humans could travel in country that was too rough for four-footed beasts of burden. Each of these men usually toted five five-gallon cans of hooch.

The liveliest area for liquor smuggling on the southern border of the United States was El Paso, Texas. It was a big city and right on the border. Just a shallow river and an imaginary line away was Ciudad Juárez, Mexico, another sizeable city. Juárez had a good highway link to Ciudad Chihuahua, a third big town. El Paso itself was the hub of a network of first-class highways in the southwest United States. Unlike most of Texas, it was a high desert town near zillions of hiding places in the sparsely populated Rocky Mountains. As its name, El Paso ("The Pass"), indicates, it was a traditional entry point to the United States.

Colonel Charles Askins, Jr. was a Border Patrolman in the El Paso area during the heyday of the Mexican bootleggers. In his *The Pistol Shooter's Book*, a treatise on marksmanship in formal pistol matches, Askins recounts some of his experiences as a Border Patrolman.[2]

"During a ten-year period, from 1924–34, the Border Patrol in the El Paso area alone," he wrote, "had an average of a gun battle every 17 days."[3] At that time, he said, the Border Patrol had 20 times more gunfights than the FBI and captured many times more dangerous criminals. But all Americans had heard about John Dillinger and "Pretty Boy" Floyd, while hardly anyone could give you the name of one Mexican smuggler.

Among the many factors that made El Paso attractive to bootleggers were the shallowness of the Rio Grande and the dense willow thickets along its banks. There was heavy brush on the part of El Paso called

Cordova Island. And just north of the river, South El Paso was a maze of narrow alleys.

Gunfights in El Paso were usually at ranges of less than 10 yards, according to Askins, and they usually happened in pitch darkness. The Border Patrol, like the previous Mounted Watchmen and Mounted Guards, was operating on a low budget. Patrolmen did not get uniforms until 1928, and their weapons were surplus from World War I.

The shoulder arm issued was the M1917 rifle called the "Enfield" because the design originated in England's Enfield Arsenal. It was a long, heavy, powerful weapon that used the .30-06 cartridge. It was accurate at more than half a mile—an excellent military rifle. But the Border Patrol agents were shooting at enemies just out of reach, not half a mile away. They were shooting at midnight, at people hiding in shadows and often completely invisible. A bolt-action rifle weighing

The U.S. Army-issued Colt .45 revolver was the standard-issue sidearm for Border Patrol (as it was dubbed in 1924) officers during and after World War I. *(Time & Life Pictures/Getty Images)*

nine and a half pounds and more than 46 inches long was hardly the ideal weapon for the close-range battles the Border Patrol had to fight.[4] The rifle's power and the penetration of its bullets made it especially unsuitable for combat in a densely populated area like South El Paso.

The issue sidearm, the Colt or Smith & Wesson M1917 revolver, was better than the rifle. Both revolvers were big, powerful weapons that used a cartridge they weren't designed to take. They were an emergency project: The country couldn't produce enough .45 automatics to meet the army's need, so the revolvers were chambered for the auto pistol cartridge, which was enough to make many patrolmen disdain them. Many of the Border Patrolmen used their own handguns, but they didn't depend on them. Their basic weapons were semiautomatic rifles, especially the .351 caliber Winchester, and repeating shotguns, usually Winchester and Remington pump guns. They paid for them out of their own pockets. They wanted firepower.

At first, the Border Patrolmen patrolled El Paso in two-man teams. They found, though, that two men did not have enough firepower, so they added another man to each team. Askins described the ideal team as having two men with Winchester .351 semiautomatic rifles and a third with a short-barrel pump or semiautomatic shotgun.

Their opponents, the smugglers, were not as well armed, but they were usually more numerous and very careful. Before night fell, scouts—teenage boys—would appear on the streets, smoking, talking, or just hanging around. If one of them caught sight of a patrolman, the planned crossing would be postponed. For the Border Patrolmen to move into position in the thickets beside the river or the alleys of South El Paso "required all the cunning of marauding Comanches,"[5] Askins said.

Sometimes the gun-toting guards the smugglers hired crossed the border early and took up positions to ambush any American lawmen that came on the scene.

"These coyotes were some of the toughest gents ever to bend a shooting iron," Askins wrote. "They were hired for the princely sum of $3.50 a night, and they knew full well what they were up against."[6] The gunmen carried a variety of pistols, rifles, and shotguns, some fairly new, and others very old. Up north, crooks and police both often carried Tommy guns. Neither group had submachine guns on the Mexican border.

If all went well, the Border Patrolmen would hear the smugglers wading through the river. When they got close, the patrolmen would rush up to them and shout, *"Manos arriba! Federales!"* (Hands up! Federal police!) The smugglers could then either drop their cargo and surrender, try to run back across the river, or open fire. The third choice was the most common.

Askins's partner in the Border Patrol was George Parker, who later became the Arizona state rifle champion. Parker had a cousin, Lon Parker, who became a hero in the force. Once, in the early 1920s, while tracking a party of smugglers who were bringing mescal (a distilled alcoholic beverage) across the border, Lon Parker heard gunfire and discovered that someone behind him was shooting at him. He turned and emptied his revolver without pausing to reload. He charged the attackers, tackled one, grabbed the smuggler's shotgun, and turned it on the other two smugglers, taking all three as prisoners. Some other patrolmen heard the shooting and ran to the spot. They found Lon Parker relaxing in the shade, holding a gun on his three prisoners. He smiled and said, "Sorry you're too late for the fun."[7]

Another time, in 1925, Lon Parker was trying to find some smugglers who were operating out of Nogales, Sonora. Someone tipped him off as to the route they took, so he and some other patrolmen set up an ambush. When three mounted smugglers driving six pack horses loaded with rum appeared, the patrolmen popped up and demanded their surrender. The smugglers galloped away, leaving the pack horses. The patrolmen unloaded the contraband and chased the smugglers.

The *contrabandistas* rode about three miles, then turned and fired at their pursuers. The Border Patrolmen returned the fire, and the smugglers fled again. Parker mounted and resumed the chase, but the smugglers had faster horses. When Parker rode back, he found that one of his companions had been killed. For the next several months, Parker devoted his own time to hunting down the killers and seeing to their arrest.

About a year after the shooting, Parker was attending a picnic with friends named Willis when a rancher told him he had seen a rider driving a train of pack horses north. It was Sunday, around 5:00 P.M., and Parker was not on duty. Nevertheless, he got on his horse and attempted to cut off the pack train.

An hour and a half later, the Willis family returned home and found Parker's body on top of their woodpile.

Parker had found the pack train and arrested the smuggler who was driving it. He didn't know there was a second smuggler until the second man, concealed behind rocks, shot him in the back with a .30-30 rifle. Parker shot the first man, then turned and emptied his .45 automatic at the second, but the smuggler got away. Parker then rode to the Willis ranch, where he died.

Several years later, the body of Parker's killer was found in the same spot where he had shot the patrolman.

The Border Patrol has a tradition of excellence in pistol marksmanship. One of the pistol champions of the past, William Henry Jordan, a retired assistant chief patrol inspector, is, like Charles Askins, also an author. Although Bill Jordan holds the highest target shooting classification for pistol, rifle, and shotgun, in his book, *No Second Place Winner*, a pistol shooting manual for police officers, he points out that not all Border Patrol shoot-outs have been characterized by deadly accuracy.

He tells of one case in El Paso where someone fired before shouting the traditional "*Manos arriba! Federales!*" The smugglers dropped their cargo and dashed back over the border. Normally, they would have gone home and prepared a new expedition.

"But this was different," Jordan writes. "Filled with indignation at what must have been considered a complete failure to observe the proper amenities, (shooting before shouting, that is) as soon as their own side of the river was reached, a hot fire was opened on the side they had just departed."[8]

The Border Patrolmen returned the fire. On the Mexican side of the line, people heard the shooting, rushed to the aid of their countrymen, and joined in the firing. All the Border Patrolmen within earshot reinforced the American officers. So did numerous citizens with no official connections. "The battle became general," Jordan wrote.

"Everybody was having a good time—beat sitting and watching a dull crossing where nothing was happening—and nobody was getting hurt to amount to anything, so the battle raged all night until daylight brought its reminders of responsibilities and the fight was mutually brought to a halt."[9]

The young Jordan was the senior Border Patrol officer present at this fracas. So when regular business began the day after the battle, he was asked to "confer" with the district director. When he entered the director's office, he was greeted with "a roar that blasted him back on his heels and which translated into something like 'I want an explanation as to why once that smuggling train was back across the river you didn't take your men and get to work instead of fooling around there enjoying yourselves all evening like you did?'"[10]

Jordan said, "I wanted to leave there in the worst way! But the fire from the other side was so intense we were hopelessly pinned down. Why, it was all a man's life was worth just to lift his head—less try to leave."[11]

The director was not impressed. He knew that Jordan had sent three details back to headquarters during the night to bring up more ammunition.

This sort of comic opera encounter was hardly typical of Border Patrol operations. More typical was the case of Senior Patrol Inspector Darwin Earle that Jordan cited to explain the necessity for a police officer to practice quick draw and rapid shooting.

On July 24, 1964, Earle, who was in charge of the Border Patrol station at Mercedes, Texas, saw a couple of men walking north from the border. He believed they were merely a pair of undocumented border crossers, so he did not draw his gun. When they passed him, he ordered them to halt. The first man whirled and fired a shot. Earle, only six feet from the gunman, was hit in the lower abdomen. The bullet went through him and struck his right hip bone. As he fell, he drew his gun and fired three shots before he hit the ground. All three shots hit the gunman, who was killed instantly. The gunman's companion ran away.

Earle crawled to his patrol car. The car was only 105 steps away, but Earle passed out several times on the way and it took him 30 minutes to make the trip. He pulled himself into the driver's seat and tried to radio for help. The car, though, was in a radio "dead spot," so Earle had to start it and move out of the dead spot. After making contact, he drove to a road and passed out again.

Earle recovered and returned to duty. He learned that his assailant was not just a "border jumper" but a thug named Cosme Cuellar

DISPUTED TURF

In his book, *The Pistol Shooter's Book*, Charles Askins told of a problem found in many government agencies, although one that was usually not potentially fatal.

He and his partner George Parker were taking a prisoner to town when they saw some smugglers crossing the border in broad daylight. They stopped the car, and Parker stayed with the prisoner while Askins went after the smugglers. He saw some wet footprints and followed the trail into a narrow alley. Askins was not prepared for serious action; he had only a two-inch barrel .38 pistol. Suddenly he saw a large man with a rifle at the end of the alley.

Askins dropped to his knees and raised the revolver. At the same time, the big man aimed his rifle. Both fired and both missed. The big man disappeared.

"I ran around some half dozen shacks trying to head him off," Askins reported, "and bumped into still another gunman, and this bird, uncomfortably enough, was also armed with a rifle. We fired together and I had the good luck to hit his gun in the small of the stock and broke it completely."

The gunman ducked behind a car, and Askins ran into the nearest house, "scaring the people inside almost out of their wits," and reloaded.

Reinforcements from the Border Patrol office arrived, but everything remained quiet. It turned out that both Askins and his opponents were federal officers. The others were Customs Service agents charged with guarding another section of the border.

"It was some of my most mediocre hand gunning, but for once I was glad of it," the future pistol champion reported.[12]

A U.S. Border Patrol agent demonstrates her marksmanship with an M-4 carbine at the Border Patrol's firing range in Fabens, Texas. *(AP Photo/Victor Calzada)*

whom the local sheriff called "the Valley's Public Enemy Number One."

The Mexican border became calmer after Prohibition. In the old days, new agents were tutored by old gunfighters like Jeff Milton. But in 1934, they got an academy.

Commenting on the new era in 1953, Charles Askins said:

Today the Border Patrol is handsomely equipped with submachine guns, Remington auto rifles, 2-way radio, Jeeps for desert travel, helicopters and a force at least ten times larger than the little band which I knew. Today recruits are sent to a training school where they are given some marksmanship training but are drilled much more strenuously on how to draw up a good

GUNFIGHTER TRADITION

Federal law enforcement agencies have acquired, justly or not, distinctive reputations. The Coast Guard is known for its seamanship with small boats; the FBI, for scientific investigation. The Border Patrol's reputation is that of wild and woolly gunfighters. It was acquired during the Prohibition era, which, it seems likely, created a "gunfighter" tradition, with more emphasis on quick-draw and point-shooting in the training of Border Patrolmen than in that of most other law-enforcers. In the 1920s and 1930s many U.S. police agencies had no firearms training at all.

The Federal Bureau of Investigation began its formal firearms training at the same time the Border Patrol did. FBI Director J. Edgar Hoover believed that if FBI agents were known to be expert marksmen, it would have a demoralizing effect on the criminal element. It would also be excellent publicity for J. Edgar Hoover. Few American public servants have ever equaled Hoover as a public relations expert.

So Hoover organized an FBI pistol team. At that time, Askins was coaching a Border Patrol team that would compete in the winter national pistol championship matches to be held in Tampa, Florida. "We heard many alarming reports about

lawyer's brief, how to interpret the immigration law, and how to make a good appearance in court. For, you see, the smuggler lost his lusty disregard for life and limb somewhere during the past decade and now gunplay along the old Rio is a relatively scarce pastime.[13]

Charles Askins was an army colonel, son of an army major; an author, son of an author; and a respected firearms expert, son of a respected firearms expert. But down deep, he was an intrepid gunfighter, a spiritual heir of Wild Bill Hickok and Jeff Milton.

this [pistol] team in the Border Patrol camp," Askins wrote, but he learned that his fears were unfounded. "When the smoke cleared away several days later, the FBI squad had garnered exactly nothing. I never heard of the team in competition after that. J. Edgar, with that fine sense of publicity values that has guided him through more than 30 years of public life, was not going to foster any aggregation which could not wipe the eye of all and sundry. The FBI Pistol Team died a borning."[14]

One by-product of the Border Patrol training and its gunfighter tradition is the many pistol-shooting champions, such as Charles Askins and Bill Toney, who have called the Border Patrol home. In 2009 Border Patrol *pistoleros* upheld their service's traditions with a near-sweep of the National Police Shooting Championships. Agent Robert Vadasz became national individual champion, beating the nearest competitor by 13 points. The nearest competitor, Enoch Smith, was also a Border Patrolman, and the third place was taken by Lieutenant Colonel John Poole, also a Border Patrol officer. Top woman competitor in the matches was Border Patrol Agent Gina Hernandez.

His judgment was a bit harsh. In the future, the Mexican border would enter a new era, one that was possibly wilder than the days of Pancho Villa.

New Professionalism

In 1934, 10 years after it was founded, the Border Patrol got an academy—the El Paso District Training School. As the name implies, the school was mostly concerned with training officers who would work in that busy part of the border with Mexico. The Border Patrol is responsible for more than 7,000 miles of land borders and 2,000 miles of seacoast, which today are divided into 20 sectors: Spokane West and Spokane East (Washington), Havre (Montana), Grand Forks (North Dakota), Detroit, Buffalo, Swanton (Vermont), Houlton (Maine), San Diego, El Centro (California), Yuma, Tucson, El Paso, Marfa (Texas), Del Rio (Texas), Rio Grande Valley, Laredo, New Orleans, Miami, and Ramey Station, which guards Puerto Rico and the Virgin Islands. Of these sectors, El Paso has historically been the noisiest.

The first class at the El Paso school contained 32 men who took four hours of class a day in Immigration Law, Spanish, Documents, Citizenship, Fingerprinting, Leadership and Duties, and Authorities of Patrol Inspectors. Three afternoons a week they practiced rifle and pistol shooting and horsemanship. They also took part in patrols. Lon Parker's superiors predicted a great future for him when he captured three undocumented aliens as a trainee on his first patrol.

In 1956 the El Paso District Training School became the U.S. Border Patrol Academy. Fourteen years later, its graduates had their official titles changed from Immigration Patrol Inspectors to Border Patrol Agents. The school also changed locations. From 1951 to 1961, it was located in six different places in the Southwest. In 1977, it became part of the Federal Law Enforcement Training Center at Glynco, Georgia.

In the late 1980s the Border Patrol experienced several spurts of growth. To train the new recruits, the service had to establish temporary training facilities at Ft. McClellan, Alabama, and the old Charleston Naval Base in South Carolina. It is now located back in the Southwest, at Artesia, New Mexico.

Border Patrol growth had been slow during the Depression and World War II due to the shortage of money in the first case and men in the second. The Great Depression began in 1929, and it brought another problem for the Border Patrolmen. In addition to chasing murderous liquor smugglers, they now had to run down peaceful farm workers and miners. The Mexicans who had been recruited during the war were now the targets of the Deportation Act of March 4, 1929. Jobs were disappearing, and there was an outcry in the country to expel foreign workers so

A Border Patrol agent and supervisor *(standing, in red shirt)* instructs a class on the proper grip and use of the Heckler & Koch P2000 handgun during the class of trainees' first day on the firing range at the U.S. Border Patrol Training Academy in Artesia, New Mexico. *(Jef Topping/Reuters/Corbis)*

more Americans could have jobs. Almost half a million people—Mexicans who had been welcomed a few years before, and even American citizens who "looked Mexican"—were sent to Mexico. The majority of that half million were American citizens. Mae Ngai, an immigration history expert at the University of Chicago, called it a "racial removal program."[1] Those who left or were removed were warned that an attempt to return would be a felony, punishable by more than a year in prison.

The anti-Mexican fervor of the Depression years had at least one odd development: Marijuana was declared illegal in 1937. Until the Depression, marijuana was known principally as an ingredient in corn plasters and veterinary medicine. It was not among the drugs like cocaine and opiates banned by the Harrison Narcotics Act of 1914. It was not banned like alcohol in 1920. But in the 1930s, a chorus of voices, mostly in the Southwest, began demanding that marijuana be banned. A Californian in 1935 wrote to the *New York Times* that "Marihuana [sic], perhaps now the most insidious of our narcotics, is a direct by-product of our unrestricted Mexican immigration. Easily grown, it has been asserted that it has recently been planted between the rows of a California penitentiary garden. Mexican peddlers have been caught distributing sample marijuana cigarettes to school children."[2]

The fear that Mexicans were taking jobs away from Americans had ignited a lot of plain and simple prejudice. Such prejudice was not confined to plain and simple people, either. According to the editor of the Alamosa, Colorado, *Daily Courier* in 1936:

> I wish I could show you what a small marijuana cigarette can do to one of our degenerate Spanish-speaking residents. That's why our problem is so great: The greatest percentage of our population is composed of Spanish-speaking persons, most of whom are low mentally because of social and racial conditions.
>
> While marijuana has figured in the greatest number of crimes in the past few years, officials fear it, not for what it has done, but for what it is capable of doing. They want to check it before an outbreak does occur.[3]

Horrible crimes were blamed on marijuana. Hordes of people seemed to believe that Mexicans lived on marijuana, and if they got rid of marijuana, they would get rid of Mexicans. As it turned out, outlawing marijuana did not get rid of either, and Mexicans smuggling marijuana into the country are now among the Border Patrol's greatest problems.

World War II brought new challenges for the Border Patrol. As in World War I, there was a manpower shortage, but it was now much more severe. At the same time, the Patrol gained new responsibilities.

At a Border Patrol office on the Mexico–U.S. border, an agent interrogates a captured illegal immigrant in 1948. *(Hulton-Deutsch Collection/Corbis)*

Among the tasks was coastal patrol. In this new area, so different from the desert most of them knew, the inspectors had both motor cruisers and inflatable rubber boats. Instead of illegal aliens, they were looking for spies, saboteurs, and submarines. Most of the Coast Guardsmen, who normally would handle this operation, were operating landing craft in the South Pacific.

Illegal aliens posed a new kind of problem. As it had done during World War I, the U.S. government tried to recruit Mexican workers to replace the Americans who had gone to war. The government brought in *braceros* (unskilled workers who have nothing to offer but their arms, or *brazos*), Mexican farm laborers, who were guaranteed a decent wage. The trouble was that American employers often passed up the opportunity to hire government-sponsored braceros, because they found they could

THE .357 MAGNUM

For the Border Patrol, which had armed its patrolmen with war-surplus revolvers, issuing them .357 Magnum revolvers was a radical change.

The .357 Magnum cartridge and revolver were introduced in 1935, the first new revolver to appear in decades. It caused a sensation in the firearms industry. It was capable of breaking an automobile's cylinder block or penetrating a car from end to end. This was the age of the automobile bandits, like John Dillinger and "Pretty Boy" Floyd, and a pistol that could do this was greatly desired by federal agents and local police.

The cartridge did not *look* like a radical improvement: It looked just like the .38 Special that could be found in the side arms of almost all the police in the United States. The .357 Magnum cartridge was, in fact, just a .38 Special that was one-tenth of an inch longer than standard. But it contained a load of powder much more potent than the load of the Special. Smith & Wesson (S&W) produced a revolver designed espe-

hire illegal immigrants for much less money. That left the patrolmen with the job of distinguishing legal from illegal Mexican farm workers.

To replace its own manpower losses because of the war, the Border Patrol hired men who had not gone to the armed forces, chiefly older men, for the duration of the war plus six months.

The Border Patrol did get some new equipment because of the war. One notable addition was a fleet of brand-new jeeps. (The Border Patrol had become nearly thoroughly motorized by this time.) The jeeps had radios, too, but that innovation was not a success. The radios used telegraph keys—not voice—to communicate. The patrolmen had to know Morse code. Further, because of the great distances they had to patrol in the Southwest, the patrolmen often found themselves closer to the headquarters of another sector than to their own.

cially to fire this cartridge, although it could also use .38 Special cartridges. The S&W revolver was a large, heavy weapon, ostensibly built of special steels. Both it and the cartridge acquired a sort of mystique. The revolver was recommended only for large, strong men in good condition. Some shooters said the noise and recoil were too great and that they wanted nothing to do with it. The price was also prohibitive, as it cost almost twice the amount of a standard, high-quality revolver. For a while, immediately after World War II, the revolver was available only to police officers.

When the dust had settled from World War II and the Korean War, Smith & Wesson and Colt began making lighter revolvers for the cartridge. These were readily accepted by both the general public and law enforcement. The Border Patrol, which by this time was on the leading edge of law enforcement agencies as far as personal armament goes, made these lighter magnums standard. Since then, the patrol has switched to semiautomatic pistols in the potent new .40 S&W caliber.

Richard Bachelor, who served briefly in the Border Patrol before leaving for the war, said, "Using those things was kind of tough, because I was stationed in South Texas and headquarters was ninety miles away. You'd begin tapping on the key, trying to raise headquarters and you'd raise New Orleans instead. Then New Orleans would have to relay your message to headquarters in South Texas."[4] Old time Border Patrolmen didn't like Morse code. Within a few weeks, most of the radios mysteriously turned up broken.

Bachelor told how the Border Patrol interned diplomats from the German, Japanese, and Italian embassies. The diplomats were kept in the Homestead Hotel in Virginia and the Greenbrier Hotel in West Virginia until arrangements could be made for them to be transported to their home countries. Seamen and other enemy nationals caught in the United States at the start of the war didn't fare so well. They went to internment camps in New Mexico and North Dakota.

Along with the new jeeps, the patrolmen got new guns—a variety of .38 caliber revolvers, including a few .357 Magnums (a kind of .38 Special on steroids that was considered by many the ultimate revolver), repeating shotguns, bolt-action rifles and semiautomatic rifles, and Reising submachine guns.

When the war ended, the Border Patrol continued its prewar activities, chiefly catching smugglers and stopping illegal immigrants. The Bracero Program continued until 1964, but the demand for illegal workers, who could be paid much less than legal workers, guaranteed a substantial number of illegal farm hands trying to cross the border.

A year after the end of the Bracero Program, Congress passed the Immigration Act of 1965. That ended the National Origins Act, which set quotas on immigrants that greatly favored those from northern and western Europe. The act of 1965 set a blanket quota for immigrants from the Western Hemisphere at 120,000 a year. By this time, Mexican immigrants were being joined by others from Central and South America.

The Border Patrol hired more inspectors, and the smugglers responded by avoiding border cities and taking to the boondocks. The Border Patrol responded by reviving the ancient art of tracking.

One of the Border Patrol's greatest trackers was Ab Taylor, who, as a farm boy, began learning the art by tracking lost cattle and wounded game. Taylor continued his education by talking to more experienced trackers and, most important, doing more tracking. Humans, he learned, were much harder to track than animals. People tried to obliterate their tracks. Taylor looked for things few other people would notice—a pebble that had been moved, a crushed piece of grass, or a thread on a bush. All these invited further scrutiny. He learned how wind or rain could alter a "sign," as the Border Patrol called anything that would indicate a human had passed that way. He frequently was on his hands and knees trying to determine the age of a sign.

To determine the age of smugglers' signs along well-traveled smugglers' routes, the Border Patrol drove jeeps towing enormous brooms to wipe out old signs as often as twice a day. Even so, the smugglers frequently had a lead of eight to 10 hours over the patrolmen. The answer then was to calculate their route, speed ahead, and attempt to "cut" the trail a short distance behind the smugglers.

Taylor became famous in the California-Baja California border country for his tracking abilities. He eventually led a picked group of "sign cutters" who were called on when the need for highly skilled tracking appeared. One case involved a little girl who had been kidnapped. The FBI was on the case, but they could find no new leads. One of Taylor's men found a heel print directly beneath the girl's bedroom window. But the FBI had so trampled the ground that he could find no other prints to match it. A week later, another of Taylor's sign-cutters found matching prints on a road heading south.

"We found the son of a bitch within a mile of Mexico," Taylor said. "He was taking that little seven-year-old girl back with him—to marry her!"[5]

A North Carolina sheriff heard of Taylor's tracking skills and arranged to take lessons from him. He then went home and made 38 felony arrests because of his new tracking skills. A year later, he sent all his deputies to train with Taylor.

The development of tracking was one result of the smugglers moving to empty spaces. Another was the return to patrols mounted on horseback, because there were some places a jeep just could not go.

In 1953 General Joseph M. Swing became commissioner of the INS. He brought a military outlook to the Border Patrol. Under him, the patrol became like the army, the "Green Machine."

"He painted everything green," Taylor said. "The buildings, the god dang cars, the uniforms. Everything."[6]

Swing also brought military equipment to the Patrol—surplus trucks, boats, even planes. He used some of the planes—C-47s, the military version of the classic DC-3—when he instituted Operation Wetback in 1954. This consisted of tracking down and deporting 1.3 million Mexicans who had been living and working in the United States, along with, in many cases, their children who had been born in the United States and were U.S. citizens. He then withdrew all Border Patrol inspectors from interior stations and put them on the border. That slowed immigration somewhat, but once an illegal immigrant got into the United States, he or she was pretty safe. The Bracero Program was still in effect, making it difficult to find any illegal immigrants without another massive effort like Operation Wetback.

Border Patrolmen were still being called on to enforce other laws—some in ordinary criminal situations, others extraordinary ones. Border Patrolman Lee Morgan became involved in one of the ordinary ones that became a bit odd. He was patrolling near Douglas, Arizona, when he heard southbound footsteps. It was only 50 yards to the border. Two men carrying bulging pillow cases appeared. They were burglars returning from a housebreaking in Douglas. Morton ordered them to stop and put down the pillow cases. They stooped down and laid the pillow cases gently on the ground. Then they stood up and brandished large knives. Morton pointed his revolver at one and told him to drop the knife and to take a couple of steps forward and lay face-down on the ground. He did. Morton then turned to the second burglar, who also dropped his knife and stepped forward.

"The only problem was that when I told him to stop, he kept coming at me," Morton said. "At the same time, like they were synchronized into each other's heads, the first burglar jumped to his knees and dove for my legs."[7]

Morton stepped back and kicked the attempted tackler, but the other crook put him in a choke hold and grabbed the cocked revolver.

Border Patrol agents guard illegal Mexican immigrants captured close to the border in June 1948. *(Getty Images)*

The patrolman kicked the first man again and tried to force the revolver back to shoot the second. The shot missed, but the concussion of the .357 knocked the second burglar off him, and Morton hit him with the pistol. He arrested both of them—not for trying to bring something into the United States but for trying to bring something out.

The odd part of this incident was when an FBI agent appeared to inquire about the case. Morton was amazed when the G-man began

TRACKING THE EXPERTS

The tracking ability of American Indians is legendary. Even in modern times, it is not unusual for western law officers to call on members of one of the Indian nations to follow the tracks of some fugitives. Ab Taylor, the Border Patrol's celebrated tracker, found that the Indians' ability to find a trail was matched by their ability to foil other trackers.

Taylor and his team were trying to find a group of Mexican Indians heading north to find work.

"They were country people who had walked all their lives," he said. "They stuck to the brush and took the time to wipe away their tracks. They were also traveling by the stars and so they didn't need to follow a straight path. They were a tough bunch—we didn't try to stay on them at night. We'd hop back on their trail in the morning, but they were traveling at such a clip we had a hard time overtaking them during the day. When we finally caught up with them during the day, they had traveled more than seventy miles. We honked our horns when we found them, to celebrate and out of respect. Believe it or not, it was the first time they had rode in a vehicle."[8]

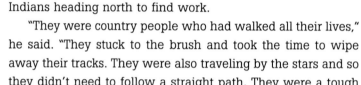

by advising him of his right to remain silent and advising him to get a lawyer. He was convinced that the government was considering charging him for kicking one burglar and hitting the other on the head with his .357. No charges were actually filed, but the two burglars were not charged with assault on a federal officer, either.

One of the extraordinary incidents was when James Meredith, the first black student at the University of Mississippi, was registering for classes in 1962. Federal officers from all over were sent to keep order at Ole Miss. One of them was the master tracker, Ab Taylor. The officers were pelted with bricks and at least one person was shooting a rifle at them. Mississippi state police did nothing. Members of the mob tried to ram the officers with a bulldozer, then a fire truck. Eventually, the government sent troops to Mississippi and ended the riot.

The Bracero Program ended two years after the Ole Miss riots, and catching illegal immigrants again became the Border Patrol's principal occupation.

Smuggling People

Coyotes became a serious problem for the Border Patrol after the Bracero Program ended. But these coyotes did not have bushy tails and howl at the moon. "Coyote" may be an insult in the United States, but it is not in Mexico. The coyote is Mexico's equivalent of France's Reynard the Fox. In Native American folklore, Coyote was the trickster god who messed up much of the Creator's work.

Being a coyote became a new profession starting in the mid-1960s. Disinviting people who for more than 20 years had been encouraged to seek jobs in the United States greatly added to attempts to illegally cross the border. A depression in Mexico in 1982, caused by the drop in oil prices, also increased illegal immigration.

Guiding contraband across the border had long been an occupation for men on the south side of the Mexican border, but as the number of people who wanted to enter the United States increased, schools for guides sprang up. Intensive education in their trade, imparted by old coyotes, made the guides true professionals.

The influx of people from south of the border revived American xenophobia to an extent not seen since the Depression. The idea of allowing persons who had lived, worked, and raised families here to become citizens was denounced as "amnesty for criminals who have broken our laws." Crossing the border illegally is, of course, a crime, but it is not the same kind of crime as robbery, rape, and murder, although some who view plans to allow illegal aliens to achieve citizenship act as if it were.

As a matter of fact, cities with large immigrant populations have shown a larger reduction of crime than cities with smaller immigrant populations, according to Barry Edmonston and James P. Smith in their 1997 book, *The New Americans: Economic, Demographic, and Fiscal Effects of Immigration.*[1] The Public Policy Institute of California reported in 2009 that this is still true today: "Cities with large immigrant populations showed larger reductions in property and violent crime than cities without large immigrant populations."[2]

Time and *Newsweek* have each run major articles about the criminal activities of Mexican drug cartels in the United States.[3] Yet ordinary violent crime has not increased in the Southwest, the part of the country that gets the lion's share of illegal immigration from Mexico. The Arizona Department of Public Safety report, *Crime in Arizona in 2009*, says that crime in Arizona in 2009 was 15 percent lower than it was during its peak in 2006 and 12 percent lower than in 2002, when it began putting crime reports on the Internet.[4] El Paso, across the border from Ciudad Juárez (one of the most violent cities in the world) is one of the least violent in the United States, with only 12 non-negligent homicides in 2009.[5]

There is a common assumption that illegal aliens do not pay taxes because people who are here illegally would not want a record of their existence, which is necessary to pay federal or state income tax. The IRS, however, estimates that 6 million unauthorized immigrants file federal income taxes every year. Many more, of course, pay Social Security taxes, which are hard to avoid because they are deducted from workers' paychecks. The Congressional Budget office says that between 50 and 75 percent of illegal immigrants pay federal, state, and local taxes. According to the *New York Times*, illegal immigrants are estimated to pay about $7 billion a year in Social Security taxes, although they cannot collect benefits.[6]

Many people have been crossing the border illegally over the years. Since 1986, the INS strategy had been based on "employer sanctions." Congress had made it illegal to hire undocumented aliens, and Border Patrol agents at interior stations were assigned to check on businesses

Former Border Patrol sector chief and current U.S. House Intelligence Committee Chairman Silvestre Reyes (D-TX) answers questions at a press conference. Reyes was responsible for planning and implementing the highly successful Operation Hold the Line in El Paso, Texas, in 1993. *(Hulton–Deutsch Collection/ Corbis)*

to ensure that they didn't hire illegal immigrants. Employer sanctions, though, were never as effective as Congress hoped. People continued to "jump the border" in large numbers.

Congressman Silvestre Reyes, a former Border Patrol official, described the employer sanctions program as "…a colossal failure, not because of the law itself, but because of the unwillingness of Congress to fund the necessary positions that would enforce employer sanctions. Those first three years that the law was in place, the assumption was that there would be no jobs because employers would comply with it. They would make sure that people had their documentation. If they had not, they would call the INS and get that issue resolved. That never happened because the INS was never given the resources."[7]

On September 18, 1993, while he was still the Border Patrol's El Paso sector chief, Silvestre Reyes stood on the bank of the Rio Grande looking at no fewer than 10,000 Mexicans and Central Americans preparing to cross the border. He was about to implement a plan that would frustrate them and future hordes of immigrants. Reyes was watching people who planned to disappear into El Paso, a largely Spanish-speaking city where most of the population had roots in Mexico. Once in the city, there would be no quick way to tell a U.S. citizen from an undocumented foreigner. Many of the Mexicans waiting to cross the border lived in Ciudad Juárez, El Paso's sister city. They held jobs on the American side of the line and they would return home in the afternoon or evening. For them, the trip across the river was a commute. The Central Americans, from Guatemala and points south, had a longer trip in mind. They would spread out to all parts of the country, where they would take menial jobs and stay for a season, a year, or forever. For both groups, though, El Paso was a magnet—once inside the city, they were pretty safe. Those planning a longer trip would have time to make arrangements.

Reyes, who grew up on a farm near El Paso, was unhappy with the situation in his native city, as were many of his fellow citizens. Talking to them, he heard many complaints about the Border Patrol. Patrolmen were harassing American citizens because they "looked Mexican." They were chasing people through the streets, roughing up people they suspected of being undocumented aliens, and causing chaos in the community. Trying to find undocumented foreigners in El Paso was not only almost impossible, it was a disaster for the whole city. Reyes wanted to try something else.

Before he returned to El Paso, Reyes was sector chief in McAllen, in southeast Texas, which had become part of a favorite route for Central Americans traveling up the east coast of Mexico. Reyes tried to get the Mexican government to stop the Central Americans from moving through its country. The Central Americans were not staying in Mexico, however; they were merely passing through and spending money along the way. The Mexicans told Reyes, in effect, that the Central Americans were his problem, not theirs.

Reyes tried something else. He arranged to have reinforcements sent to the McAllen sector, stationing them on the river so they could guard every conceivable route to the north. Patrolmen were on guard 24 hours a day. The would-be immigrants found that there was no way to get over the border, so they stayed on the south side of the border, crowding Mexican cities and causing problems. After a while, Mexico set up check points on its southern border and slowed the flow of people from Central America.

Now in El Paso, where the immigration problem was much bigger, Reyes planned a similar operation. Holding the El Paso sector would take many more men. The Border Patrol had greatly expanded by 1993, but it was finding that it still needed more agents. Reyes's plan, Operation Blockade, would require a lot of agents. They would be lined up along the river so closely that each agent would be able to see the agents to the left or right. Behind the line of agents on the river, Reyes would have a mobile force of 100 agents who could be rushed to stem any attempt at a mass breakthrough.

To sell the operation to his superiors, Reyes proposed three benchmarks. The first would come when the blockade had been in force 72 hours. He estimated that it would take that long for the would-be border crossers to realize that there was no way to sneak over the line in the El Paso area. They might try to induce Reyes to call off his troops by blocking the bridge to prevent Americans from entering Mexico. But if they did, the troops would stay anyway. They might try to rush the agents, but that would bring the mobile force up to stem the tide.

The second benchmark would come in a week. People on the American side would not be able get the employees they had been depending on. They would complain, but the guards would stay in place, because the complaints would prove the blockade was working.

The third benchmark would come in 30 days, when the extra money appropriated for Operation Blockade would run out. If the Border Patrol hierarchy was happy with the way immigration was affected, Operation Blockade could be made permanent.

The Border Patrol measures the extent of illegal immigration by the number of apprehensions. In fiscal year 1993, the El Paso sector had 285,000 apprehensions. The next year, the number dropped to 79,000, which reflected a sharp drop in the number of people attempting to cross the border. The Border Patrol brass and the INS were happy and Blockade became permanent, but with its name changed to Operation Hold the Line. The Mexican government objected to the name Blockade, which in international relations is the name for an act of war.

The people of the El Paso area were even happier. They elected Silvestre Reyes to Congress.

In 1994 in the San Diego sector, another area with heavy illegal immigration, Sector Chief Gustavo De La Vina modified Operation Hold the Line to suit his sector's geography—high, steep mountains and deep canyons—and called it Operation Gatekeeper. Again, the traffic of illegal immigrants dropped sharply. Gatekeeper added another touch: De La Vina got the navy to build a fence with surplus metal landing mats, used to quickly build air strips on islands in the South Pacific during World War II. De La Vina later became chief of the Border Patrol.

The coyotes and pollos shifted their operations to Arizona. So did the Border Patrol, where it established another Hold the Line clone, Operation Safeguard.

Illegal immigration began to flow heavily into really desolate areas—stark desert and mountains. The Border Patrol tried to lower the tide with a collection of high-tech tools. In 1991 the Office of National Drug Control Policy, one of the agencies concerned with securing the national border, had commissioned Sandia National Laboratories (which develops science-based technologies that support national security) to recommend methods of improved border surveillance. The Sandia Study

The MQ-9 Predator B drone, an unmanned surveillance aircraft system, takes off at Libby Army Airfield at Fort Huachuca in Sierra Vista, Arizona. *(Getty Images)*

recommended remote control cameras, television, electronic sensors, and fences and other barriers. In addition, the Patrol used helicopters and light planes. Currently, it also uses unmanned drones like the latest ones based in Afghanistan.

In spite of these tactics, crowds of people are still crossing the Mexican border without papers.

Coyotes and their pollos often cut fences, allowing cattle to roam away from ranches; they leave garbage on private property; and sometimes they steal private property. On at least two occasions a smuggler illegally crossing the border is suspected to have murdered a rancher.[8]

In their book, *On the Line: Inside the U.S. Border Patrol*, Erich Krauss and Alex Pacheco tell of Roger Barnett, who owns a 22,000-acre ranch

VIGILANTE DRONES

One of the vigilante groups that line the border looking for illegal aliens has unmanned reconnaissance planes, operating on the same principle as the drones used by the military and the U.S. Border Patrol. The vigilantes call themselves the American Border Patrol but they are, like the better-known Minutemen, a private organization and have no connection with the U.S. Border Patrol, which is a U.S. government agency.

According to Glenn Spencer, head of the vigilante group, his organization has two of the unmanned aerial vehicles to look for unauthorized border crossers. The drones are equipped with global positioning devices so that the vigilantes can tell the U.S. Border Patrol the exact position of any illegal immigrants the drones find.

These privately owned drones seem to be a bargain-basement version of the military's and Border Patrol's unmanned planes. The drones cost $5,000 and have a wingspan of only five and one-half feet. Unlike the high-flying government drones, the vigilante group's drones fly at an altitude of only 300 to 400 feet, which is beneath the 500 feet mandated for aircraft that need certification by the Federal Aviation Administration. Spencer says the aircraft were made by members of his group who had experience in electronics.

Mario Villarreal, a spokesman for the U.S. Bureau of Customs and Border Protection, said, "We appreciate the community's efforts to notify us of suspicious activities . . . We encourage them to call the Border Patrol or law enforcement, but these efforts should be within the law."[9]

in Cochise County, Arizona. On one trip around the ranch, he found a cattle gate left open, a section of wire fence cut, a water pipe broken and spouting a geyser 12 feet high, and garbage and abandoned backpacks strewn all around. All of this had happened in the week since he had last been in this part of the ranch.

Barnett says 300 to 500 illegal immigrants cross his property every day. He knows this because he patrols his property with a rifle and a dog every day. When he finds a group of illegal aliens, he covers them with his rifle and calls the Border Patrol on a cell phone. In 2002, he apprehended 2,200 border jumpers. Barnett spent $2,500 on electronic sensors to monitor the most frequently used routes across his land, but the aliens have not stopped coming. One time, they stole one of his trucks for the trip north.

"Ten years ago, there was no problem down here," he said. "Six years ago there was no problem—you didn't see it. But in the last five years [since 1998], it has gotten totally out of control."[10]

Barnett has gotten a reputation among the coyotes. Some of them are now avoiding his ranch, but he heard that some of the drug syndicates have put a price on his head. "A lot of people think we shouldn't have guns because we don't need guns," he said. "Boy, let me tell you, down here you better not go out without one."[11]

Barnett thinks the United States should station soldiers along the border, but the military is forbidden from civilian law enforcement by the Posse Comitatus Act of 1878. The act forbids the federal military from enforcing civil law, but it does not apply to state troops, the National Guard. It is a reaction to what were considered the excesses of the military during the Reconstruction that followed the Civil War. In 1989, though, because of the growing drug trade, the border was approaching the level of bloodiness it saw during Prohibition, so the law was temporarily waived. Joint Task Force 6, composed of the Air Force, the Army, and the Marine Corps, was established to provide intelligence for the Border Patrol. If a member of the task force saw something illegal, he was to inform the Border Patrol so an arrest could be made.

On May 20, 1997, four marines from the task force saw someone carrying a rifle. They began stalking him, staying out of sight as much as possible. They were about 200 yards away when they saw him level his rifle at something in their direction. They fired. And then they learned they had killed an American teenager. The kid was trying to round up the family goats and had fired his .22 rifle at a rock or something nowhere near the marines, who had been mostly out of his sight. Stationing armed combat troops on the border has since stopped.

Several vigilante groups have sprung up ostensibly to aid the Border Patrol in its effort to catch undocumented aliens. The best-known of them, the Minuteman Project, claimed as many as 1,000 volunteers patrolling the Arizona border. They seem to be, at best, a mixed blessing.

A May 2005 report prepared by the minority staff of the House of Representatives' Committee on Homeland Security had this to say about the Minutemen: "Volunteers filling the role of trained law enforcement officers raise a number of safety concerns—both for the volunteers and for Border Patrol and other law enforcement agents charged with securing our borders.

The Minuteman Project permits its volunteers to carry weapons, creating a heightened risk of violence. While the Minuteman Project claims that their volunteers are on the border solely to observe and report illegal activity, overly aggressive volunteers could attack unarmed, undocumented immigrants in an act of vigilantism. Armed

Minuteman volunteers armed with binoculars and pistols watch the Mexico-United States border for any signs of illegal immigrants trying to cross the border near Bisbee, Arizona. *(David Howells/ Corbis)*

BORDER GUARDS—OFFICIAL AND UNOFFICIAL

The U.S. Border Patrol appreciates the help it gets from citizens in locating illegal activity, but it does not consider the Minutemen or any other volunteer group a Border Patrol auxiliary. It is concerned about the rights of illegal aliens in the border area and the possibility that unofficial border watchmen may violate those rights.

The Border Patrol has agreed to notify the Mexican government as to the location of volunteer border watchers when they participate in apprehending illegal immigrants or if violence has been used against border crossers.

Mario Martinez, a U.S. Customs and Border Protection spokesman, said that such notification is standard procedure to reassure the Mexican government that the migrants' rights are being protected.

"This . . . simply makes two basic statements—that we will not allow any lawlessness of any type, and that if an alien is encountered by a Minuteman or arrested by the Minutemen, then we will allow that government to interview the person," Martinez said."[12]

volunteers could also encounter a dangerous person, such as a drug trafficker. The exponential growth in the number of violent incidents involving Border Patrol agents in the area known as the Tucson Sector underscores this point. This sector averages one assault incident every two days. At that pace there will be an increase of 80 percent in violent incidents in 2010. While Border Patrol agents are trained to deal with such situations, the Minutemen and similar groups are not. Untrained volunteers could also place Border Patrol agents at risk by creating dangerous crossfire situations or by causing Border Patrol agents to be distracted.[13]

One of the problems armed volunteers could cause became apparent when Carlos Ibarra Perez, known as a Mexican civil rights activist, in June 2000 announced a $10,000 reward for anyone who killed a U.S. Border Patrolman. His reasoning was that if U.S. citizens were arming to kill Mexicans, why shouldn't Mexican immigrants kill Americans? Ibarra Perez later denied that he had made such an announcement, but his belief, which is shared by others, shows the danger Border Patrol agents face.

Another problem is that armed volunteer groups have accidentally activated sensors, creating false alarms.

Estimates of the number of undocumented aliens in the United States vary from 11 to 20 million. Most authorities put the number at 12 million, give or take a million, as nobody can be sure. One reason there are so many, a reason that is seldom discussed, is that it is so hard to get into the country. Back when the braceros could come to the United States for seasonal work and then return home, there was no such population of permanent aliens. Today, once illegal immigrants get into the country, many are unwilling to go home and then face the same problems they had on their initial trip to the United States.

Keeping undocumented aliens out of the United States has never been easy, and it has gotten a lot more complicated since professional smugglers started bringing them in. The smugglers include some of the same violent individuals who sneak drugs across the border. They have little regard for any human life but their own—they could not care less about the Border Patrol agents or their clients.

The "Bandit Teams"

On December 27, 1976, a woman named Rosa Lugo and her 13-year-old daughter Esther were hiding in a drainage tunnel that crossed the border under the fence. The woman and her daughter were among 20 other pollos waiting for their coyotes to take them to the Promised Land. It was dark and cold and scary in the tunnel, but Rosa thought next year might be different and her daughter would have a chance at a new life.

Then a gang of teenage street thugs from Tijuana burst into the tunnel. They scattered the pollos, grabbed the little girl, and began to tear off her clothes. She screamed, her mother screamed, and the thugs ignored them. Rosa Lugo began to pray. She asked God for a miracle to save her daughter.

Suddenly she heard someone yell "*Sabes que?*" ("Know what?" in English.) Then a shout of "Barf!"

Swinging blackjacks and waving guns, a group of San Diego police officers and Border Patrolmen crashed through the mob.

"Sabes que?" was the San Diego police code for "Get ready," and "Barf!" from the team leader meant "Get them!"

The boy bandits tumbled out on to the street with the police in hot pursuit. When the melee was over all the teenagers had disappeared—all but the would-be rapist who had been stripping Esther Lugo. The team leader, Manny Lopez, felt someone grab his hand and begin kissing it. It was Rosa Lugo, who seemed to think Sergeant Manny Lopez was an angel sent from God.

The team of city police and Border Patrolmen was the brainchild of a former Border Patrolman and current San Diego police lieutenant named Burl Richard Snider.

In the early 1970s, before the big influx of illegal immigrants began, Snider was living in San Ysidro, California, and he was bothered by what he saw. San Ysidro is not an incorporated town. It's a run-down neighborhood within the San Diego city limits. San Ysidro was hardly a rich place, but it was almost paradise compared to what was on the other side of the U.S.-Mexican border. Snider felt that he was living on the edge of the Third World. He was living, as cop-turned-author Joseph Wambaugh put it, "in the richest half of the richest state in the richest nation in the whole world."[1]

Across the border was the city of Tijuana, formerly called Tiajuana, a town grown from a hacienda named for somebody's Aunt Juana, to the capital and largest city of the impoverished state of Baja California Norte. Tijuana is a boomtown that had absorbed its neighbor, Agua Caliente. In the 1930s, Caliente was much better known than Tiajuana. Caliente was home to the only gambling casino convenient to the affluent citizens of Southern California. San Diego has almost a million inhabitants, many of them affluent. Tijuana is about the same size, but nothing about Tijuana is affluent—it is a place where a stroll of a few blocks beyond the tourist-trap main drag can involve stepping over a dozen drunks prostrate on the sidewalk. Only the kingpins of the drug cartels are affluent there. Tijuana is a place where people die of cholera, polio, typhus, tuberculosis, and rickets—diseases that are uncommon north of the border.

As Snider saw it, the Mexican border was a line not so much between two nations as between two economies. Snider's family had been migratory farm workers ("Okies" in California slang), although they came from Missouri. He learned Spanish from Mexican farm workers' kids, and then studied it in school. The "Okie" understood the "Beaners" (derogatory slang for Mexicans). And he understood why people living south of the border would want to come north.

"I kept thinking, what if I'd been born a hundred yards south of that invisible line? As long as it's the haves and the have-nots side by side, they're going to come."[2]

He left the Border Patrol and, after working as a park policeman in Washington, D.C., returned to San Diego and joined the police force. In 1976, he was a lieutenant in the force, and the great northward migration had begun. San Diego was a gateway to the rich farms of the Imperial Valley, to those of the Central Valley and to the enormous city of Los Angeles. Snider was even more disturbed by what he saw than in his San Ysidro days.

A third group was crossing the border with the pollos and the coyotes. They had no animal name. They were not like the wily coyotes or the helpless pollos. They might be compared to wolves, but that would insult the wolves. They deserved to be called *cabrón* (meaning "big goats" literally, but a deadly insult in Mexico). Like the other two groups of Mexicans, they were border-jumping to better themselves, but how they did it took neither the skill of the coyotes nor the courage and endurance of the pollos. All it took was moral depravity. They came to rob, rape, and murder their fellow citizens, who had illegally crossed the border, where they would be safe from Mexican law.

The San Diego police began finding bodies in the desert canyons that were within the city's limits. Some of them were women and children. The women usually had been raped. These bandits relied on terror. If they came upon a group of pollos, they might grab one man and mutilate him with knives to terrorize the rest of the group before they even demanded money. The pollos were easy targets. They carried their life savings with them for food and bus fare; they couldn't afford firearms, which are anyway unavailable legally to ordinary people in Mexico, and they were afraid to speak to the American police, because they would be deported. So for the bandits there was gold in the hills and canyons of rural San Diego.

It drove Snider crazy. No one seemed to care. The victims, after all, were illegal aliens. Then something happened that made Americans, especially those in Washington, more aware of Mexico. In the 1970s the king of Saudi Arabia decided to limit the export of oil. The embargo resulted in long lines at gas stations, rapidly rising prices for gasoline

Border Patrol agents seize and arrest illegal immigrants crossing from Tijuana, Mexico, into San Ysidro, California, in 1977. The 1970s saw a rise in Mexican bandits that terrorized fellow Mexicans that had illegally crossed the border into the United States. *(Tom Nebbia/Corbis)*

and heating oil, and efforts by Presidents Jimmy Carter and Richard Nixon to limit U.S. oil consumption. Mexico produced oil, and it didn't worry about what some king on the other side of the world decided. Mexico's friendship was important, so even officials who didn't share Snider's humanitarian views thought something should be done about the thugs who were preying on Mexicans at the border.

Snider began conducting a one-man publicity campaign. He walked the canyons himself; he checked police records, and he took the stories he gathered to the news media. His stories were gory enough so that even the most blasé had to agree that something should be done, but what?

San Diego police knew little about cactus-studded mountains, rattlesnake-filled canyons, scorpions, tarantulas, and other dangerous wildlife. They were used to traveling in squad cars through lighted streets, not navigating in a desert when there was no moon or stars, when dark was not just dark but totally black.

Snider knew that terrain from his days on the Border Patrol. He thought the city police and Border Patrol agents could form a task force to clean the bandits out of the hills. The Border Patrolmen could navigate and the police could make arrests. Snider pushed the idea, and his statements appeared in the press or on television as often as three times a week.

"Here's a picture of a 14-year-old girl when they finished with her . . .," he would tell his television audience. "Here's what they did to a man

TWO-GUN MEN

Some people may be puzzled as to why Border Patrolmen on the Bandit Teams often packed two handguns. Modern pistolmen deride the two-gun cowboys seen in the movies and on television. They allow as how there may have been people who carried two revolvers in the days of the cap and ball handguns (revolvers in which gunpowder and bullets were loaded separately and touched off by a percussion cap mounted on the cylinder) or even in the early days of metallic cartridges. Cap and ball revolvers were often jammed by fragments of the exploded cap, and if that happened, it was nice to have another gun ready to go. Early metallic cartridges were also unreliable, and a bullet stuck in the bore or at the junction of the cylinder or barrel could also put a revolver out of action. Guns like the famous Single Action Army Colt, featured in many Western movies were slow to reload. That could be inconvenient if the shooter had to take more than six shots.

Further, "practical" pistol shooting, as taught in most police organizations today, generally dictates that both hands should

who didn't have enough money to satisfy them...."[3] He described one atrocity after another.

Journalists began asking both city and federal authorities about the possibilities of a combined Border Patrol/Police task force. And so it happened: Federal and city officers were combined in the Border Alien Robbery Force, which the Border Patrol agents referred to as the Bandit Teams. The earthier officers preferred an acronym—BARF.

Both elements of the Bandit Teams knew that their operations would be quite different from anything they had done before. David Krohn, who had spent four years fighting in Vietnam before joining the Border Patrol, said the situation was completely different for the

hold one pistol. Nobody has four hands. Why should anyone need two pistols?

Border Patrol agents, heirs to a long gun-fighting tradition, had their reasons. They carried one revolver and one automatic. Because of the shape of its handle, the revolver is easier for most people to grasp and draw. All modern service revolvers are double action: There's no need to cock the hammer or release a safety catch before firing. That makes it very fast for the first shot. Pulling the trigger revolves the cylinder and brings a new cartridge in position and then fires it. If the first shot is a dud, a second shot can be fired instantly, which means the revolver is reliable. The pseudo-pollos keep their guns in their pockets. If necessary, a revolver can be fired repeatedly from inside a pocket. An automatic would jam after the first shot.

Why did they also carry automatics? Automatics are loaded with magazines. All service automatic magazines carry more cartridges than most revolvers—in some cases more than double the number of cartridges. Equally important, dropping a used magazine and inserting another can be done much faster than loading six cartridges into a cylinder.

city police. "The police officers were used to having their radios up and calling in. They're used to high visibility. The Bandit Team detail was very low visibility."[4]

The visibility was lower than even the Border Patrol agents were used to.

"As a Border Patrol agent," Krohn said, "you sit back and watch the bandits go back and forth across the border. Because we patrolled in marked vehicles, we couldn't sneak up on them—we couldn't catch them in action. I knew what kind of things were going on out there . . . Part of the reason I wanted on the team was for revenge. Many times I had come across aliens who had been robbed and women who had been raped. I wanted to do something."[5]

Everybody knew this detail would be dangerous. The Border Patrol agents carried two guns, usually a revolver and a semiautomatic pistol. The revolvers were generally medium-sized .357 Magnums like the Smith & Wesson Combat Magnum or the Colt .357. The revolvers were more powerful, ultra-reliable, quicker to draw, and very fast for the first shot; the automatics held more cartridges and could be reloaded almost instantly. Pistols were the main weapon because they could be easily concealed. One member of a team, though, carried a short-barreled shotgun to provide serious firepower. The shotgun was usually a High Standard Model 10, a 12-gauge police model that had a flashlight mounted on top and a pistol grip at the balance point so it could be fired with one hand.

The city police relied mostly on their issued revolvers—.38 Specials with two-inch barrels—easily concealed, but not notably powerful. But they, too, usually had a team member with a shotgun. The San Diego officers were not as well armed as the Border Patrolmen and they seemed to have a different view of weapons. Sergeant Manuel Lopez, leader of the police team, admitted he didn't know a thing about guns and ammunition. Wambaugh points out that "Most policemen, though they carry handguns as tools of their trade, are not technically versed in firearms."[6]

In one respect, a most important one, the local police had a big advantage over the Border Patrol agents—low visibility. Except for two members of a support team, they were all Mexican-Americans. Most of them spoke some Spanish. That Spanish, though, included the slang of San Ysidro and Tijuana, which might not be intelligible to a native of Jalisco or Panama. And the pollos the Bandit Team was trying to imitate came from Jalisco, Quintana Roo, Durango, and all Mexican states as well as from other countries like Guatemala, Nicaragua, and Panama. Even so, the police had less trouble passing than most of the Border Patrol.

At first, though, nobody seemed to worry about visibility. The Bandit Teams went out wearing black watch caps, goggles, and military camouflage fatigues. Nobody was going to take these commando clones for Mexican or Central American peasants. The city of San Diego had given the Bandit Teams 90 days to accomplish something. They quickly understood that the way to get bandits is to attract them, and to do that, they had to look like potential victims, not storm troopers.

A typical night of patrolling began with the Bandit Team members gathering in their Chula Vista station in their pollo outfits. Pollos normally wore two or three layers of clothing so they wouldn't have to carry suitcases. Then the pseudo-pollos would all clean their weapons and pass them around for the others to inspect, emulating the Border Patrol's method of carefully handling weapons before going out on the job. Then they would hike out to the immigrant trails and wait for bandits to come along. When anyone approached they would crouch down as the pollos did—a posture of submission. The strangers might be other immigrants, coyotes looking for paying customers, or bandits.

One night, Krohn and his team—two other Border Patrol agents and three police officers—saw three men approaching. One of them was carrying a paper sack. Not being a Mexican-American, Krohn stayed back in the shadows where he couldn't be seen.

"Where are you going?" one of the strangers asked in Spanish.

"Waiting for our guide," one member of the team answered in the same language.

"We could take you north?"

The team member declined, saying they had already made arrangements.[7]

The strangers walked on.

As the strangers turned away, Krohn got a good look at the paper sack. He was sure it held a gun.

LEARNING TO BE A CHICKEN

One of the hardest tasks, especially for the very macho San Diego police officers, was acting like a pollo. The people crossing the border to find a new life had been continually oppressed in their old lives. They had been put down by landlords, officials, gangsters, and police. Whenever a stranger approached, they saw potential trouble. They instinctively adopted a posture of submission, a kind of cringe—sort of crouched down and bent over.

It was not enough to look shabby, like the average pollo. The lawmen had to adopt the pollo's posture and ape his attitude. They had to cringe like an illegal alien even when they were sitting down. The patrolmen and the police had ample opportunity to learn the pollo cringe. They were authority figures, and to poor Mexicans, an approaching police officer was usually a threat. It was not unusual for a Mexican police officer to charge an innocent person with some violation of the law and then ask for a bribe to forget it. The *mordito* (little bite—a bribe) was a way of life for underpaid Mexican police.

The Border Patrolmen and police officers learned the pollo posture well. Even when they pretended to be Central Americans but spoke border Spanish, they looked enough like genuine pollos to fool the bandits.

No threat had been made, so there were no grounds for arrest, but Krohn was full of suspicion. He told the others he thought they should follow the three. They did. Any action was better than sitting in the dark and hoping for something interesting.

About 100 yards ahead, they saw the three again. The man with the paper sack was pointing a gun at some cowering pollos while his companions were slapping and kicking the would-be immigrants. A woman was trying to hide in the background. Krohn thought the bandits were planning to rape her. The Bandit Team suddenly jumped out of the underbrush behind the bandits, knocked them down, handcuffed them, and took them away. The immigrants continued traveling north.

Things got quiet for the anti-bandit patrols as winter approached. The city began to lose interest. It looked as if the Bandit Teams would have to disband when they passed the city-imposed deadline of 90 days. On December 27, just two weeks before the deadline, the Bandit Team members rescued Rosa Lugo and her daughter. The "Miracle in the Tunnel" made a good story for the television and newspapers, but it didn't save the Bandit Teams. Richard Snider was disconsolate. He revived his publicity campaign. Manny Lopez said the lieutenant was taking the wrong approach:

"Saving people? Helping *illegal aliens*? The police administration laughed at Snider behind his back. When I was director of the San Diego Police Officers Association, I had to work with the brass and the politicians every day to get what the cops wanted. . . .You don't get things done *helping* illegal aliens. I talked about City Hall and how if we could reinstate BARF, I'd guarantee we'd get the kind of press relations to make them give anything the department wanted in our next budget request. That's how you accomplish your goals in the real world."[8]

The bandits helped, too. When the Bandit Teams stopped operating, the number of violent incidents at the border increased dramatically. Snider and Lopez made sure the media knew it. Mayor Pete Wilson, who was planning a race for the U.S. Senate, didn't like the publicity. In three weeks, the Bandit Teams were reinstated.

Back in action, after watching processions of coyotes and pollos hike north, Krohn and his team moved close to the line to see if they might attract some bandits there. They saw two men crawl through a hole in the fence and approach them. The pseudo-pollos squatted down and waited. One of the newcomers lighted a cigarette and strolled over to them.

"Where are you going?" the smoker asked. "Heading north? The border is dangerous these days. Need a guide to take you north?" He dropped his cigarette and ground it out. When he raised his hand, it held a gun. He didn't know that the "pollos" all had their hands on guns in their pockets.

"So many shots were fired at the same time it was like the Fourth of July," Krohn said.[9] The armed bandit fell flat. His companion dashed for the border, but the Bandit Team caught him before he could cross the line. The felled bandit didn't die, and the Mexican government identified him: He was a former police officer from Mexico City. He had come to Tijuana to join the police force there. The other bandit they captured was his brother. They were robbing aliens to get enough money to buy a police uniform.

Some of the bandits, the Bandit Teams learned, were not just ex-police officers; they were working police officers from Tijuana moonlighting for extra money. As time went on, robbing would-be immigrants who had crossed the border became a much less attractive business.

One of the San Diego police teams got into a shoot-out with a couple of Tijuana police who were not trying to rob aliens. The Mexican police saw Manny Lopez's team lurking near the fence that separated the two nations. The Mexican officers thought the American police were would-be immigrants. They yelled to the "pollos": "Return to Mexico." The "pollos" didn't move. That was not the way pollos behaved. They didn't identify themselves, either. They didn't want to blow their cover. The two Mexican police were now convinced that the "pollos" were really bandits. They crossed the border to get them. Now the American officers thought the Mexican police were really robber-police. At the last second, Lopez decided to identify himself. He yelled *"Policia,"* and lifted both hands. He had a badge in one hand and a gun in the other.

"He's got a gun!" one of the Mexican officers, Pedro Espindola, yelled. The other Mexican policeman, Chuey Hernandez, drew his gun. Everybody—seven Americans and two Mexicans—began firing. The two Mexicans were severely injured and one American was somewhat less severely wounded.

(opposite page) The wall marking the border between the United States and Mexico runs across the Mesa de Otay shantytown on the Mexican side in Tijuana, Mexico. Expansions to the wall and other measures to control illegal immigration have been on the rise since the implementation of Operation Gatekeeper in the mid-1990s, resulting in a decline in illegal crossings since 2000. *(AFP/ Getty Images)*

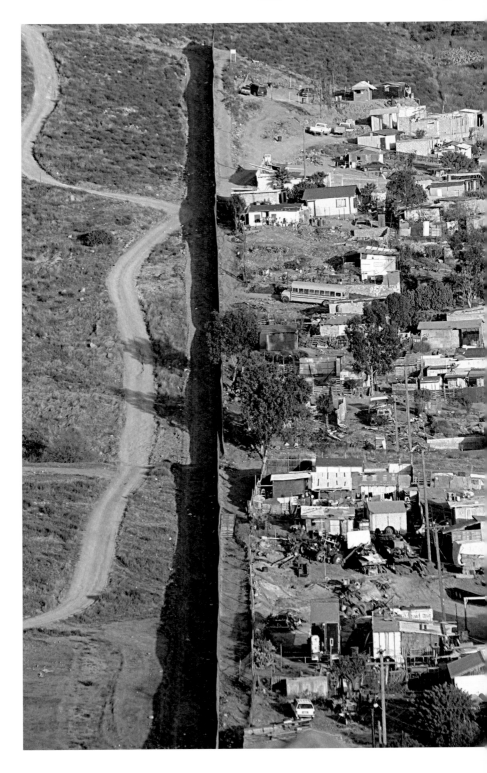

Machismo met machismo—Mexican machismo in crossing the border and Mexican-American machismo in refusing to let the other police know who they were until it was too late. The result: an international incident that did nobody any good.[10]

In spite of that, the Bandit Team experiment was working.

"When we started out," Krohn said, "bandits were robbing aliens as much as twelve miles north of the border, but after only a few months, we had pushed the bandits back into Mexico."[11]

The Bandit Teams were finally disbanded in April of 1978. The bandits quickly came back, but the political pressure was too much for the bandit hunters. They were being accused of being cold-blooded killers of Mexican citizens by the Mexican government, which didn't seem to care that anyone the teams killed was definitely a cold-blooded killer of Mexican citizens and was killed only in self-defense. Probably more important in ending the program was the criticism by Americans, who were outraged that American law officers were letting illegal aliens into the country because they were too busy arresting rapists and murderers.

As a result murder, rape, and robbery returned to the canyons and grew worse and worse. The area attracted miscreants from all over Mexico. They were more ruthless and better armed. In the past, some bandits relied on knives and big rocks they picked up from the ground. Now almost all of them had guns. In 1984 the San Diego police and the Border Patrol established a new task force, the Border Crime Prevention Unit (BCPU).

Manny Garcia, one of the first police officers recruited for the BCPU, said:

> I served in the army, but that didn't give me any idea of what it would be like out there. It was very different. We were police officers *and* Border Patrol agents and we were not supposed to be fighting a war—but in many ways we were. It had just gotten to the point where the laws of California *had* to be enforced. So administrators said, "Let's go back there, but this time, let's be more organized." In order to do this, we relied heavily on the Border Patrol. The area was pretty treacherous out there, and the Border Patrol knew where all the trails and dangers were.

Once the Border Patrol had scoped out the entire area, they brought in the officers and trained them. The Bandit Team had been a kind of ragtag outfit that went undercover. We were more formalized and highly supervised.[12]

Garcia had a dangerous job. He had been born and raised in Mexico. He spoke Spanish like a Mexican, because that was what he was—not someone with a Spanish name and distant roots in Mexico. He was a point man, the guy who walked in front and was the spokesman for his team. There were two teams, each with three Border Patrol agents and three policemen. Because some Mexican civil rights activists charged that the Bandit Team members were guilty of entrapment, the BCPU officers wore uniforms and badges.

That was not as big a handicap as it might seem. It gets very dark in the desert, and after years of no law enforcement there, the bandits got very bold. Garcia said, "One of my fellow agents was squatting down, looking for bandits through his night vision glasses. He didn't see anything, so he took them off—but it takes a few minutes for your eyes to adjust. When his vision finally focused, there was a guy right beside him with a rifle, pointing it at him. Because the agent was squatting down, he drew his gun, fell to his back and started shooting. I think he hit the guy twice in the leg before he took off, running toward Tijuana."[13] Garcia, in the mobile unit at this time, found him lying on the ground a few hundred yards from the shooting and put him in an ambulance.

Captain Sing of the San Diego Police Department, commander of the BCPU, brought in George Williams, a police tactical specialist, to make his men more effective in gunfights. Williams decided that the men fired too fast, considering where the gunfights took place. The muzzle flashes of their guns tended to blind them in the dense dark of the desert.

"Before I came in," Williams said, "each team was expending over 100 rounds per shooting, and many times they didn't hit anything. When you fire as fast as you can, after two or three rounds, you are blind. Then it is pure luck."[14]

Williams trained them to fire no faster than one shot a second. "They began shooting with dead-on accuracy," Williams said. In the two weeks following their training, the crime-preventers had three gunfights. On each occasion, two or three suspects were shot dead. In the 36 months the BCPU teams patrolled the canyons, they averaged a shooting every three and a half weeks.

As always, there was criticism of the lawmen in the desert. Latin American civil rights groups bashed them in the press for killing Mexicans in the canyons. But the view of the illegal immigrants was quite different. One night, the BCPU had a gunfight near the border with some bandits. Watching were thousands of pollos, preparing to "jump the border" as soon as it was dark enough. When they heard the shooting, they ran to the fence. "Kill them!" they shouted to the police. And when the bandits were bleeding on the ground, they cheered.

As before, the most potent criticism came from citizens who cared less about killing the murderers and rapists and more about letting crowds of undocumented aliens into the country. Letting them get robbed, raped, and murdered might discourage some who thought about illegally coming to the United States. The desert patrols were again discontinued.

In 1994 the San Diego Sector copied El Paso's Operation Hold the Line and instituted Operation Gatekeeper. Gatekeeper greatly reduced the hordes crossing the border in search of a better life in the San Diego Sector. Now the hordes moved east and tried to cross some of the most forbidding country in the United States, resulting in many more bodies in the wilderness and new problems for the Border Patrol.

BORSTAR and BORTAC

On April 1, 2001, Border Patrol agents spotted five people sitting along the side of Interstate 8 in California. They looked like pollos—very ragged pollos. The agents stopped, and the pollos did not run. They didn't have enough strength to run. They were overjoyed to see the patrolmen. They had been in the mountains when a storm struck. For two days they slogged through freezing rain and snow. They had no food, no guide, and they thought they were going to die. The storm was continuing when the agents spotted the immigrants. In fact, it was increasing and had already dumped two feet of snow on the ground. The agents let them into the patrol car and gave them water and blankets. They said that more members of their group were located a quarter of a mile down the trail. They didn't have enough strength to reach the road.

By this time the snow was blinding. The agents radioed for help. The call was taken by a special Border Patrol unit that had been organized in San Diego a short time before. It was called BORSTAR for Border Patrol Search Trauma and Rescue. The BORSTAR agents had been expecting a call like this as soon as they heard that the storm was approaching. They had been organizing their equipment, readying foul weather clothing, and studying maps. Their helicopter was on standby. They located the other group of pollos, all of them suffering from hypothermia and needing medical attention. They learned that there were more pollos farther back on the trail. After getting this group on the chopper and on

Members of the BORSTAR team attempt to save the lives of illegal immigrants suffering from heat stroke and dehydration. *(Andrew Holbrooke/Corbis)*

the way to safety, they looked for more. It turned out that they belonged to a large group of illegal immigrants that had become scattered in the storm. The BORSTAR agents called the San Diego County Search and Rescue and the U.S. Coast Guard for more helicopters.

As the Coast Guard pilot was flying to the nearest hospital, he saw still another group—13 persons—stranded on a mountaintop and called the BORSTAR agents. The agents set out immediately, but when they reached the immigrants one of them had already died of exposure. Then the Search and Rescue helicopter arrived. The BORSTAR people suggested that the new helicopter investigate some locations where more pollos might be found. Reports of people stranded in the storm continued to come in.

"We started at two o'clock in the morning, and I don't think we pulled out of there until late in the evening the following day," said Keith Jones, one of the BORSTAR agents. "There was one guy—his feet were so frostbitten that they started a fire sometime during the night, and he had put his feet up against the fire and actually melted his shoes to his feet."[1]

It was a hard day's night for the BORSTAR crew. They saved 31 people, and there were nine dead.

The San Diego Sector already had a Regional Emergency and Crisis Team (REACT), which is now part of a national team, the National Special Response Team (NSRT). NSRT agents handle a wide variety of crises, such as helping to restore order in New Orleans after Hurricane Katrina. Cases like the mountain rescue, though, required fairly sophisticated medical help as well as such skills as rock climbing and rappelling from helicopters and, sometimes, rescuing people drowning in rapids. They could best be handled by a new group of specialists. And BORSTAR was born. The idea spread to the whole Border Patrol.

The desert around San Diego was a harsh environment, but the immigrants who walked those trails were usually only minutes away from a city of a million people with all kinds of facilities. The desert trails later immigrants took were not near anything. As the illegal immigration routes shifted from El Paso and San Diego to the boondocks, BORSTAR units had to be set up along most of the Mexican border.

Because their work—saving lives—is so gratifying, there are always many more applications for membership in BORSTAR than openings.

LIFE AND DEATH IN THE BOONDOCKS

When the Border Patrol made a special effort to block traditional smuggling paths around El Paso, San Diego, and Tucson, the coyotes smuggling drugs and people took other, non-traditional routes. Each smuggler had his own idea of a good way to evade the border guards.

The best way to avoid apprehension is to take a route through an area where no one lives. The downside of this is that no one lives in those areas because no one *can* live there. Those are places with no water and no roads, with high, rugged, trackless mountains. There are a lot of places like that along both the southern and northern U.S. borders, which poses a serious problem for the Border Patrol. It cannot pick a few places to concentrate its efforts: The United States has more than 7,000 miles of land border.

Another problem is, of course, that it is easy for people on foot to get in trouble crossing these desolate and uninhabited areas. That is especially a problem for BORSTAR.

To be admitted to BORSTAR, an agent has to have two years of service as a Border Patrol agent and then must pass a three-stage selection process. The first stage, as is usual for "elite" units, is physical fitness.

The fitness requirements for some agencies, including another Border Patrol group, BORTAC (Border Patrol Tactical Unit), are said to be rigorous. But the BORTAC fitness test—40 pushups and 60 sit-ups in under two minutes, 7 full pull-ups and a mile-and-a-half run in under 11 minutes—would be a cinch for a graduate of ordinary infantry basic training. That is not true of all of the BORSTAR training.

Before becoming a BORSTAR agent, a trainee must run 12 miles carrying a person on a medical litter. This is a team test, and BORSTAR trainees are grouped into five-man teams. How many agents carry the litter for how long and how they are picked are team decisions. Team-

A couple of generations ago, the problem was almost unsolvable. The answer now is aircraft, especially helicopters. Planes can rush qualified BORSTAR agents to the area, and helicopters can get them to the scene. Helicopter rescue was pioneered by the U.S. Army during the Korean War, and it has been highly developed since. In Korea, an injured person was placed on a litter that was fastened underneath one of the small helicopters used then. The patient got a lot of fresh air on the way to a field hospital. Today's helicopters are big enough to allow a patient to lie inside. They don't even have to land. They can hover above the scene of the trouble and lower a basket to bring the patient up. BORSTAR medics can also get to a patient while the aircraft is hovering, by doing what the government calls rappelling, which is a way of sliding down a rope. It is not an art recommended for the faint-hearted or those with a fear of heights.

BORSTAR has cut down the number of deaths in desolate places at the border, but the most sophisticated rescue equipment is useless unless the Border Patrol knows that someone out there is in trouble.

work is vastly important. Most situations the trainees encounter involve teamwork. Sometimes the mock patients complicate things by resisting all help.

Keith Jones said, "It gives them (the trainees) an opportunity to see if they can think on their feet and adjust to changes in the situation. The strength of the team originates from our ability to work together, and we need to select individuals who can work as a team, especially when they get tired. When things get a little difficult, their true personalities tend to come out."[2]

After the field tests, the trainees have an oral interview and then go to Camp Pendleton, the Marine Corps Base, for basic training. The day begins with physical training such as running an obstacle course and lap swimming. Also in the swimming pool, they learn how to rescue drowning persons and how to keep from drowning themselves. There is classroom work on search and rescue fundamentals and basic EMT (emergency medical technician) skills. In the field, they learn map reading, compass navigation, and the use of GPS (global positioning satellites). They learn how to rig litters and "package" patients for various kinds of evacuation, such as helicopter. They also learn aircraft safety, aircraft marshalling, and landing-zone safety.

Like the army's Special Forces (Green Berets), the BORSTAR agents specialize. Specialties include technical rescue, medical, navigation, communications, and operations.

"We send our guys to a lot of different training, from the private sector to the military. We're constantly training," Jones said. "Our technical rescue team, for example, will go through the Marine Corps helicopter rope suspension training class. Every time we send somebody to training, they will bring that knowledge back, share it with the team, and we will decide if we want to incorporate it into our program."[3]

On their day-to-day work, the BORSTAR agents spend most of their time patrolling trouble spots. Those are the dangerous areas where immigrants are likely to freeze or die of dehydration, to fall into ravines, or collapse from exhaustion climbing mountains. The agents are seldom comfortable. Their fingers and toes freeze, they are soaked in icy water, or they are tortured by thirst. They use their tracking skills to follow pollos who have become lost or have been abandoned by the coyotes they paid. Some pollos are elderly; some are toddlers. Almost all are near death. Some are dead when they are found.

While patrolling, Border Patrol Agent Jacob Rissman noticed tracks that indicated the man who made them had been injured. He followed the tracks and eventually found a 70-year-old man curled up in the bottom of a ravine. The man had sprained his ankle and could not keep up with his group. The ankle got worse and eventually he could not walk. By the time Rissman found him, the old man had been at the bottom of the ravine for three days under a scorching sun. He could not even scream.

Rissman called BORSTAR, which sent a helicopter. The BORSTAR chopper dropped a basket and flew the man to a hospital, where he was treated and recovered.

Not all the people BORSTAR rescues are illegal immigrants. Some are tourists. One, for instance, was a four-year-old boy who had become

A Border Patrol BORSTAR supervisor checks a campsite for signs of recent occupancy by illegal immigrants in Avra Valley, southwest of Tucson, Arizona. Hundreds of people die every year in their attempt to cross the desert. *(Rick D'Elia/Corbis)*

separated from people on a park-sponsored tour of the Anzo-Borrego Desert in California. It was winter, and night temperatures dropped rapidly. BORSTAR was notified, and their agents found the boy's tracks. When the tracks disappeared, they brought in their canine unit. Two hours after they began the hunt, the agents returned the child to his parents.

Some of those rescued are Border Patrol agents. "A lot of the time, our agents will experience heat exhaustion," said Keith Jones. "They're wearing all the equipment, they are tracking, it gets hot, and before you know it, they run out of water, and they're in an area that's not very accessible. . . .We assisted an agent who had an anaphylactic reaction to some of the plant life out in the east county. We've had broken ankles, you name it."[4]

Would-be immigrants die not only in the deserts and mountains of the United States, but also in similar terrain south of the border. Mexican officials estimate that more than 2,000 have died on both sides of the border since the establishment of Operation Hold the Line. Because of the deaths in Mexico, BORSTAR agents have been sharing with Mexican officials what they have learned about saving people stranded in desolate parts of our country.

The Border Patrol's other elite group, BORTAC, also operates in foreign countries. What the Special Forces are to the army, BORTAC is to the Border Patrol—an elite unit that can be sent anywhere in the world to handle special situations. And like the Green Berets, their assignments are often classified.

The origins of BORTAC go back to the Mariel Boat Lift in 1980, when Fidel Castro offered to release dissidents and political prisoners who wanted to come to the United States. The United States agreed to take them, but American authorities did not expect what they got.

No fewer than 120,000 Cubans boarded boats at the Cuban port of Mariel and began arriving in south Florida. Nobody in the U.S. government expected such a horde of refugees, although it had been practically an article of faith in Washington that just about everyone on the island wanted to get away from Castro. What to do with these "Marielitos" posed a new problem for the United States. The INS immediately rounded them up and interned them, promising to process them and release them to family members or sponsors in the United States.

Finding sponsors was easier said than done. Castro had released not only political prisoners but also burglars, con men, cutthroats, drug users, drunks, and as many undesirables as he could crowd onto boats to the United States. Not surprisingly, there was a dearth of sponsors for crooks and madmen.

Castro would not take them back, so the Marielitos stayed in overcrowded American jails while the INS tried to think of what to do with them. Federal courts held that the interned Cubans had no constitutional rights as they had landed illegally. It should have surprised no one that the Marielitos began rioting in their detention centers, located all over the country. The Border Patrol, the principal INS law enforcement agency, had to cope with the riots. The Border Patrol organized regional teams to handle the riots. The regional teams, however, had their own individual procedures and protocols. The riots were big enough to require the attentions of more than one team, and that produced problems, such as who was in charge and how some situations should be handled.

Riots in federal detention facilities were a specialty of the U.S. Marshals, not the Border Patrol. To learn more about what to do in such riots, the Border Patrol sent some of its agents to the U.S. Marshals for training with the Marshals' Special Operations Group. Forty volunteers were selected from 200 applicants and spent the next five weeks training 17 hours a day in rappelling from helicopters, practicing martial arts, marksmanship, and crowd control formations. They learned land navigation, operations planning, and advanced weaponry.

Twenty-four agents completed the training and were given special equipment—body armor, helmets, and various weapons, all packed in a bag. They were told to keep those bags with them at all times. Whatever their regular duties were, they were now on call 24 hours a day to go to emergencies. When called, they were expected to be at an airport, with their bags, purchasing airline tickets within half an hour.

It was only two weeks after they finished their training that the first group of Marshals-trained Border Patrol agents, now known as BORTAC, got a call. Although most of the Marielitos had been released, large numbers of them had violated their paroles and were back in jail. Those at the KHROME Service Processing Center, a detention center in Miami, Florida, rioted again.

The Border Patrol agents went into the lockdown areas and took people out in small groups. Other agents got the facility staff to identify the ringleaders. They separated them from the general population and sent them to other facilities where they were not known and would have a hard time starting new riots.

New riots started, though—new riots in old places like, yet again, the KHROME detention center a few months later. The Border Patrol agents

NONLETHAL WEAPONS

BORTAC agents have a variety weapons to break up riots, especially at detention centers. The rubber shotgun pellets used at the KHROME detention center are an example. These should not be confused with the "rubber bullets" used by police and security forces to break up demonstrations in some foreign countries. Those "rubber bullets" have a diameter of 20 millimeters and are 2 or 3 inches long. They can easily kill at short range. The "bean bags" used at the KHROME center are bags filled with plastic pellets and usually fired from a special projector. The concussion grenades are less powerful than military concussion grenades. They are nicknamed "flash bangs," and their most noticeable effect is a tremendous noise and a large, brilliant flash.

Tear gas is an old, reliable antiriot weapon. It can be used in a grenade that suddenly bursts or in one that ignites and burns comparatively slowly, spewing gas from holes in the grenade body. There are also tear gas cartridges that blow a cloud of tear gas out of a gun designed for such use.

Large security forces can break up a riot by marching into a crowd in a V-shape formation with nothing more sophisticated than batons.

All of these weapons, including the batons, can be misused in ways that make them fatal. The Border Patrol trains its agents intensively so that nonfatal weapons stay nonfatal.

of BORTAC returned, this time with shotguns firing rubber pellets and "beanbags." The Marielitos had already set fire to their barracks and were breaking into the women's section when the BORTAC agents arrived. The nonfatal but painful missiles drove them back. Then the Border Patrol agents shipped them off to other federal facilities, their old barracks having burned to the ground. Most of them went to the Federal Detention Center at Oakdale, Louisiana, or the Federal Prison at Atlanta, Georgia.

Years passed, and the public forgot about the Marielitos. Then on November 20, 1987, the U.S. Department of Justice announced that the United States and Cuba had reached an agreement. Cuba would take back the imprisoned Marielitos. The Marielitos went crazy. Cuba was the last place they wanted to be.

Eight BORTAC agents from the New Orleans Sector confronted some 200 surly Marielitos at Oakdale soon after getting a call.

"We tried to prepare all day for what we believed would be an eventual attack by the inmates," said Robert Coleman, one of the BORTAC agents.[5] At 5:00 P.M., the prisoners tried to rush the gate. The Border Patrol agents threw tear gas grenades at their feet. The inmates fell back but later recuperated from the gas and charged again. The BORTAC agents were running out of gas, but they got concussion grenades and frustrated another charge.

More BORTAC reinforcements arrived, as well as deputy sheriffs and Bureau of Prisons officers. The Marielitos couldn't get out, but the officers couldn't get in, either. The Oakdale situation turned into the longest prison siege in U.S. history, with the Marielitos holding 26 hostages, FBI agents negotiating with the inmates, and BORTAC agents guarding the perimeter.

After nine days, the prisoners and the FBI reached an agreement. If the prisoners released their hostages, the FBI promised that all of the Cubans would have a fair hearing and a chance to say why they should not be returned to Cuba. The BORTAC agents prepared to go home, but two days later, the Marielitos in Atlanta rioted.

"Oakdale is the place in the United States where we send the worst of the worst before we send them home," said Lynne Underdown, who was appointed assistant district director for detention and deportation in the New Orleans District. In 1992, Underdown was the first woman patrol agent-in-charge in Border Patrol history.[6] When she joined the Border Patrol in 1980, she knew every woman in the service—all 20 of them. Today there are hundreds.

The Marielito riots were a turning point for BORTAC. The Border Patrol decided to give this elite group full backing. It sent people to train with other federal agencies like the FBI and the DEA. BORTAC agents began working with the military to learn and use the latest advances in weaponry. They began working on a wide variety of missions. For instance, some of them went to Bolivia to hunt down the jungle laboratories that make cocaine paste out of coca leaves.

The BORTAC agents used helicopters and light planes to find the labs. "A cocaine laboratory is not easy to spot," said Kevin Oaks, commander of BORTAC. "It's basically just a hole in the jungle. They build big, long maturation pits out of sticks and whatnot. They dump the leaves in there, and then they add precursor chemicals used to activate the alkaloid in the coca leaf. They put men in there wearing rubber boots, and they'll stomp in these *poso* pits for 12, 15, 18 hours, chewing on that coca leaf so they can stay awake. Then they do one or two more processes to turn it into what they call "*queso*" (cheese), which are these little balls of paste cocaine."[7]

To locate these jungle laboratories, the BORTAC aerial observers would look for landing strips in the jungle. They would land, then fan out in the jungle and usually discover a network of small labs. After they and the UMOPAR (the Bolivian antidrug police, known as the Mobile Police Unit for Rural Areas) destroyed the labs, they would blow holes in the airstrip to make it useless.

BORTAC's presence in Bolivia was a training mission. They showed the UMOPAR how to use aerial reconnaissance to find jungle labs and how to set up checkpoints to intercept shipments of precursor chemicals and coca leaves. The Bolivian project was followed by other, similar jobs in other South American countries. In Central America, BORTAC helped local police forces locate and intercept drugs en route to the United States.

The North Country and 9/11

On December 14, 1999, a young Algerian who said his name was Benni Noris drove off a ferry traveling between Victoria, British Columbia, and Port Angeles, Washington. To Diana Dean, the U.S. border control agent at Port Angeles, he looked "hinky." He was also extremely nervous. The young man, whose real name was Ahmed Ressam, had been cleared by U.S. officials in Victoria, but Dean decided to search his car anyway. She found that he had much to be nervous about: The vehicle was full of explosives, including nitroglycerine, timing devices, and more bomb-making materials. When Dean asked to see more identification, Ressam tried to flee and was arrested.

He admitted that he was planning to set off a major explosion at Los Angeles International Airport around January 1, 2000. The so-called Millennium Bomber's attack was one of several attack plots planned for that date, all of which failed. This was more than a year before the September 11, 2001, attack.

Ressam had not tried to sneak through the woods on the Canadian border, nor did he attempt to trudge across the desert on the Mexican border, which would have been a neat trick with a load of nitroglycerine. He used forged passports and phony names, methods available to a large and well-financed organization like Al-Qaeda but not to a

Guatemalan peasant. For anyone with access to the resources of Al-Qaeda or a similar terrorist group, Canada offers much easier access to the United States than Mexico.

For most of its history, the Border Patrol has focused on the Mexican border. There are several reasons.

First, Mexico is a much larger country than Canada. With more than 100 million people, Mexico is the largest Spanish-speaking country in the world.

Second, the Mexican Revolution produced more than 20 years of violence and lawlessness, which created an atmosphere conducive to more violence and lawlessness.

Third, there is extreme inequality in the distribution of wealth in Mexico and in much of Latin America. For instance, Carlos Slim, said by *Time*, ABC News, and CNN Money to be the world's richest man, lives in Mexico. Slim owns 8 percent of Mexico's entire gross domestic product. The average annual income for a worker in Mexico is $2,000, and a worker in the poorest 40 percent of the population makes only $550 a year. The economic situation in the small countries in Central America is at least as bad as in Mexico. There are huge numbers of poor people in those countries. Many of them want to come to the United States to get better-paying jobs. A few remain at home and turn to crime, such as smuggling.

None of these conditions are present in Canada. The United States border with Canada extends for 5,525 miles compared with the 2,000-mile border with Mexico and the 2,000 miles of coast around Florida and Puerto Rico. The Canadian border is almost three times as long as the border with Mexico, and it, too, includes mountainous areas, along with sparsely populated plains. The border area also includes dense forests and the Great Lakes and the St. Lawrence River. And if the northern border has fewer scorching deserts, the south lacks the frozen wastes of Alaska. For awhile, early in the Prohibition era, the Border Patrol sent more officers north than south. Violent confrontations with Mexican smugglers reversed that trend.

The Mexican border still has the vast majority of the more than 20,000 Border Patrol agents currently staffing the agency. There are drug smugglers in Canada, too, as well as some illegal immigrants. In spite of the talk of terrorists shaving off their beards and jumping the Mexican border, only three known terrorism suspects have entered the country from Mexico, and they didn't hike through the desert to get there. More have come from Canada. The best-known terrorists here—the 9/11 hijackers—flew directly to the United States carrying visas. Ahmed Ressam, however, the so-called Millennium Bomber who planned to set off a bomb in Los Angeles, drove into the state of Washington in 1999, from British Columbia. According to Janet Napolitano, secretary of the Department of Homeland Security, several other suspects have since come to the United States via the northern land route. Secretary Napolitano's statement ruffled some Canadian feathers. Commentators accused her of saying Mohammed Atta and his 9/11 crew entered the United States from Canada, but she said her remarks had been misinterpreted.

The secretary has firsthand experience with national borders. From 2003 to 2009, she was governor of Arizona, currently the scene of the heaviest illegal traffic from Mexico. Congress has authorized walls and fences to be built along various parts of the U.S.-Mexico border. Some segments of it have been built; others have yet to be constructed. The fence would not be continuous. Gaps in it would be covered with remote control television cameras and other sensing devices. Its effectiveness has been doubted. When she was governor of Arizona, Secretary Napolitano once said that if a 50-foot-high fence were built, she wouldn't be surprised if someone south of the border soon had a 51-foot ladder. Other officials have criticized the fact that the barrier will run through private property, preventing property owners from entering their own land.

Janet Napolitano's current bailiwick, the Department of Homeland Security, is the prime participant in the task of guarding U.S. borders. Homeland Security, created in 2002 in response to the 9/11 attack, is a combination of a number of federal agencies. The Homeland Security Act disbanded the Immigration and Naturalization Service and divided its functions into the U.S. Citizenship and Immigration Services, U.S. Immigration and Customs Enforcement, and Customs and Border Protection. It placed all three of these organizations into the Department of Homeland Security. The Border Patrol became part of Customs

Border Patrol agents ride their ATVs looking for signs of illegal aliens as they patrol the border between the Canadian territory to the right and Beecher Falls, Vermont, to the left. *(Getty Images)*

and Border Protection. Top priority was given to preventing terrorists and terrorist weapons from entering the United States, although the Border Patrol still spends most of its time preventing smuggling and illegal immigration. Actually, terrorists have shown little preference for wandering through the southwestern desert and not much more for the land route from Canada. International terrorist organizations are well-heeled, and their agents have used safer and more comfortable ways to enter the country. Terrorists aside, illegal traffic is much lighter from Canada than from Mexico. In 2008 Border Patrol agents on the Mexican border made 705,005 arrests, while on the Canadian border, arrests came to only 7,925.

UNARMED DRONES PATROL CANADIAN BORDER

Unarmed drones, first used to watch the Mexican border, are now also patrolling the Canadian border. The aircraft, "piloted" by Border Patrol agents at ground stations, with the aid of television, are one more step in beefing up the U.S. northern border. The drones are similar to the unmanned aircraft used in Afghanistan and Pakistan, except that they carry no rockets, guns, or bombs.

The first Border Patrol drones were Israeli-made aircraft that could fly as fast as 90 miles per hour. The current, American-made unmanned planes, called the Predator B, are built by the General Atomics Aeronautical Systems in San Diego. They can fly 260 miles per hour for 18 hours. They usually hover at 15,000 to 20,000 feet, but can fly as high as 50,000 feet. At that altitude they are undetectable to anyone on the ground lacking the most sophisticated equipment.

Drones are also being used for sea patrol. They can spot surface craft, low-flying planes trying to fly under the radar, semi-submersible boats, and small submarines, one of the newest methods drug smugglers have adopted to get their products to the United States.

The Predator's cameras can transmit pictures even at night. They cooperate with manned helicopter and can "light up" targets with infrared light invisible to anyone who does not have the night vision glasses worn by the helicopter crews who can then intercept the target individuals.

On the Canadian border, the Predators are unusually helpful over the Great Lakes region, which has a large volume of undocumented traffic.

Nevertheless, the Canadian border, like other Border Patrol jurisdictions, has benefited from considerable beefing-up since the creation of the Homeland Security Department. Between 1986 and 2002, funding for the Border Patrol had increased by 519 percent and staffing by 221 percent. The government has made a $20 million contract with Boeing to set up 16 new video surveillance towers in Michigan and New York, primarily to monitor maritime traffic on the Great Lakes, Lake St. Clair, and the Niagara River.

Mark Borkowski, executive director of the Secure Border Initiative at Customs and Border Protection, said the cameras could be used to zoom in on a boat that left Canada and watch everywhere it goes. "So the idea is to have cameras watch, and then agents are freed up to respond," he said.[1]

Four similar cameras have already been installed in the Buffalo area. The northern border's security measures also include unmanned drones like those now in use in Afghanistan and Pakistan.

Not all additional security measures along the Canadian border are high-tech. Horses made a comeback along the Mexican border when smugglers and illegal immigrants took to the boondocks to avoid heavily patrolled metropolitan areas like El Paso and San Diego. The northern return to mounted patrols has a cost-saving aspect, as well as utilization of an existing natural resource. The horses are mustangs from the Bureau of Land Management. As of 2010, the Bureau has too many of these wild horses and is afraid it may have to euthanize some of them. The mustangs are native to the Western United States and their ancestors have been living there since the early Spanish explorers brought horses to the New World. They are adapted to the terrain and the climate. They have big bones and big hoofs and can go places other horses cannot.

The horses recall old times on the frontier, but the rest of the Border Patrol's equipment is state of the art. In spite of a budget that has been at times slim, or even parsimonious, the agency's technology has been surprisingly cutting-edge in some areas. In the 1930s, it used autogiros, a now almost-forgotten aircraft that used an unpowered rotor and a conventional airplane propeller. It could take off and land in an extremely small area, although it could not rise and descend vertically

9/11, TERRORISTS, AND CANADA

In an interview in April 2009, Janet Napolitano, secretary of the Department of Homeland Security, remarked that terrorists had entered the United States from Canada, causing a minor uproar in Canada. Some commentators charged that Napolitano had revived the "9/11 myth," which is that the aerial hijackers who caused commercial airliners to crash into the World Trade Center towers and the Pentagon on September 11, 2001, had entered the United States from Canada.

The diplomatic kerfuffle caused the Homeland Security secretary to issue a statement on April 14. Napolitano said she knew full well that the 9/11 terrorists landed in the United States, not Canada. But, she said, "There are other instances, however, when suspected terrorists have attempted to enter our country from Canada. Some of these are well known to the public such as the Millennium Bomber, while others are not due to security reasons.

"Yes, Canada is not Mexico, it doesn't have a drug war going on, it didn't have 6,000 homicides that were drug-related last year. Nevertheless, to the extent that terrorists have entered our country across a border, it's been the Canadian border."

She added, "The fact of the matter is that Canada allows people into its country that we do not allow into ours. That's why you have to have a border and you have to have border policies that make sense."[2]

like a helicopter. In the north, the Border Patrol uses snowmobiles to go where even mustangs cannot. The patrol keeps an eye on both borders with unmanned aircraft, some of which are more advanced than many of the drones the military is using in Afghanistan and Pakistan.

Some of its weapons are also, arguably, more advanced than those used by the military. Its issue pistol, the basic weapon of the Border Patrol agent, until recently had been the Beretta 96D, similar to the

Beretta 92F that had been adopted by the U.S. military—except that the 92F uses the 9mm Parabellum cartridge and the 96D uses the much more powerful .40 caliber cartridge (using a bullet four-tenths of an inch in diameter). Now the issue pistol is the brand-new Heckler & Koch P2000, also in .40 caliber. The agents still rely on a repeating shotgun, the 12-gauge Remington 870, and a submachine gun, the Heckler & Koch UMP in .40 caliber. Both are appropriate for the close-quarters gunfights the Border Patrol gets into, although the army uses the shotgun only for special situations, and the submachine gun is almost obsolete. The Border Patrol rifle, however, is the same as the army's M-4.

The Border Patrol needs the latest in weaponry, because recent developments on the southern border pose a new clear and present danger—clearer and much more present than either illegal immigration or terrorism. The drug cartels in the northern states of Mexico have long tentacles—reaching all the way to Alaska. And the leaders of those cartels have demonstrated the sort of power and ruthlessness that make the notoriously violent Pablo Escobar, the late Colombian drug lord, look like an altar boy.

The Cartels

Senior Patrol Agent Alex Pacheco and his partner, each in separate cars, were waiting in the dark along a frequently used smugglers' trail in Arizona when Pacheco heard the sound of vehicles approaching. It did not sound like the easily replaced jalopies smugglers use. This was the noise of two powerful, well-tuned diesel engines.

"While scanning the horizon, I remembered a bit of news I had received years before. . . . On March 14, 2000, two Mexican military vehicles had blazed over the barbed wire fence marking the international border and drove onto U.S. soil near Santa Teresa, New Mexico," Pacheco wrote later. "A patrolman roaming nearby attempted to inform the nine heavily armed soldiers in the lead vehicle that they were no longer in Mexico. The soldiers' response had been to open fire on the federal agent and chase him for more than a mile north of the border where a bizarre Mexican standoff occurred."[1]

The patrolman had stopped when he reached a Border Patrol horse barn. The Mexicans stopped and brought out their weapons. The patrolman drew his pistol and radioed for help. The agents in the horse barn saw what was going on and asked the local police for help.

Meanwhile, another Border Patrol agent, this one on horseback, saw the second Humvee and told the soldiers they were not in Mexico. They drove their Humvee directly at him. In this vehicle, too, there were nine soldiers. Realizing the odds were against him, the mounted patrolman turned his horse into rocky country that would impede the Humvee.

The soldiers demanded that he surrender, and when he did not, they shot at him. Then another mounted agent appeared. The Mexican soldiers started to chase him, but he, too, took his horse into rough

PEONAGE IN THE UNITED STATES

In Mexico, peons were farmers who worked land belonging to someone else, usually one of the rich *haciendados* (property owners or proprietors). The peons's labor was in lieu of rent money. They were allowed to raise their own crops, but they could only work on them after the sun went down. They could not leave the hacienda without permission, and they could trade only at their hacienda store. As a result, they were always in debt and condemned to work for the *haciendados* perpetually—a condition they passed along to their children. A medieval serf had more rights than a Mexican peon.

Peonage is now illegal in Mexico, but the cartel masters have instituted a new form of it in the United States. Illegal immigrants have to pay large fees to the coyotes—most of which goes to the cartels—who guide them across the border. These pollos, of course, do not have that kind of money. They pay it in installments after they settle in the United States. If they do not pay, they may be kidnapped or murdered. In some cases, the pollos do not get a chance to settle in the United States. They are imprisoned in a house owned by a cartel and their relatives are forced to pay in order to keep them alive.

Those are ordinary illegal immigrants. There is also a specialized branch of human smuggling that the cartels have moved in on—it used to be called "white slavery," but today it is known as human trafficking. Basically, it is the trafficking of young women, mostly from Eastern Europe and Southeast Asia, who are forced to work as prostitutes to pay off the fees charged for bringing them into the country. And the fees for all "exotics" (non-Latinos) are enormous.

With the billions they have made smuggling drugs, the cartels have been able to corrupt officials and to branch out into other forms of criminality.

country, and the Mexicans soon found their Humvee stuck on a sand dune. Then several police cars appeared, like the U.S. Cavalry in a western movie. The Mexican captain in command ordered his men to lay down their weapons and explained that he thought they were still in Mexico. The American officers looked in the Humvee, but it was not carrying drugs. Nobody searched the second Humvee before it was towed off the sand dune and departed for Mexico. Could it have been carrying drugs? The agents still speculate on that.

Pacheco was thinking about this incident and wondered if the approaching vehicles were Mexican Army. He and his partner agreed to turn on their lights if the approaching vehicle were Mexican military and let the soldiers know they were U.S. agents.

The Border Patrolmen saw approaching headlights, but then the headlights went out. Then they saw the silhouettes of two Humvees approaching. The lead Humvee crossed the border and stopped in front of Pacheco's car. Pacheco turned on his overhead light. He leaned out of the window and in Spanish told the occupants of the Humvee—four Mexican soldiers in uniform and armed with automatic rifles—that they were now in the United States. The Humvee started to back up. Then it stopped, and the second Humvee joined it. Suddenly the soldiers in both vehicles began firing bursts of full automatic fire that churned up the ground around the two Border Patrol cars.

Pacheco and his partner had only pistols. They were facing eight soldiers with machine guns. The only result of a firefight would be two more Border Patrol agents killed. They backed up and headed north. The Mexicans then went back into Mexico.

The Mexican soldiers may have been on an ego trip, taunting the Americans, or they may have been trying to clear the area for drug smugglers. Or they may have been transporting drugs themselves and decided that all the shooting may have triggered American reinforcements. Any time Mexican military are found across the border, their only explanation is that they are lost. There have been many such occasions. In their book *On the Line*, which was published in 2004, Pacheco and Krauss say there were 118 incursions by Mexican military that have been recorded.

It is well known that the Mexican drug cartels have many police on their payrolls. It is hardly inconceivable, then, that the cartels have been able to corrupt some soldiers, too. The corruption of police agencies is extensive. José Reyes Ferriz, the mayor of Juárez since 2007, has attempted to purge the city's corrupt police force. He has already fired half of the city's police force, but it's an uphill job. In April 2009 a police captain in Juárez was arrested for helping one of the cartels. He was accused of arresting people on the mob's hit list and turning them over to their murderers. The corruption has extended into the federal government. A former federal antidrug czar has been arrested for taking $450,000 for supplying intelligence to the Sinaloa Cartel, currently one of Mexico's biggest.

Life in Juárez is dangerous for honest police. Fifty of them were murdered in 2008. In February the police chief resigned after the cartel informed him that it would kill a police officer every 48 hours until he left office. Reyes has asked the federal government for federal police and soldiers to help police Juárez's streets. It has helped. The city's murder rate has dropped from 10 a day to five. At the same time Reyes is trying to hire 2,000 more police officers, who will be paid $9,000 a year to start—twice what Mexican municipal police officers normally get.

In contrast, El Paso, just across the river from Juárez, with the majority of its population of Mexican descent, is one of the safest cities in the United States. Last year it had 16 murders. Juárez had 1,600.

In the 1980s the biggest drug kingpins in the Western Hemisphere were Colombians. Colombia was plagued by an almost-incessant civil war, which, like the Mexican Revolution, produced a thriving criminal class. People like Fabio and Jorge Ochoa and Pablo Escobar shipped dope to the United States by air and sea. For a number of reasons, not the least of them the U.S. Coast Guard, the air and sea routes became increasingly hazardous. So they made arrangements with the Mexican gangsters who were already making millions smuggling Mexican-grown marijuana.

The Mexicans were old hands at smuggling into the United States, and they did not have the same troubles as the Colombians. In 1983 the Colombian government declared war on the drug cartels. Cocaine laboratories were destroyed; cartel leaders were hunted down and imprisoned or killed. In contrast, the Mexican drug traffickers had government protection. The Institutional Revolutionary Party (PRI),

KILLED IN ACTION

For a historically small law enforcement force, the Border Patrol has had a lot of its agents killed in action: 109 since the Watchmen was founded.

Almost one-third (30) of those killed died from hostile gunfire. Two more were stabbed to death, and 14 died in aircraft accidents, one of them in an autogiro crash. Four drowned, the sort of accident that seldom happens to city policemen, but city policemen seldom have to rescue people in the wilderness. Three agents were deliberately run down by cars or trucks, and three more were accidentally struck and killed by motor vehicles. Two more were killed in car chases and one in a motorcycle accident. Three were struck by trains, another accident that seldom happens to most people, but most people seldom have to deal with vehicles stuck on railroad tracks.

Auto accidents are much more common, and almost as many Border Patrol agents died from this cause as from gun assault. Two died in motorcycle accidents. Three of them died from accidental shootings. Three agents suffered fatal assaults that involved neither guns nor knives.

One agent died from heat exhaustion, a hazard for people who work in the Southwestern desert. Falls are another hazard for those who work in the mountains. Four agents died in falls. Six had heart attacks and one died of "duty-related illness."[2]

which was founded during the Mexican Revolution and ruled Mexico for 70 years, accommodated, but regulated, the drug trade. The Mexican smugglers made their own arrangements with the South American cocaine producers and more or less took over the smuggling of both cocaine and marijuana into the United States.

Then in 2000, the PRI lost the presidency. Now *nobody* was regulating the drug trade. Cartels split up into factions and fought over turf. Mexico in normal times had a murder rate *five times* that of the United

States. Since the drug wars began, the murder rate has gone from one of the worst in the world to almost unbelievably high. From the beginning of 2008 to April, 2009, Mexico had 7,000 drug-related murders. El Paso's sister city, Juárez, alone had almost 2,000.

In 2006, when Felipe Calderon became president of Mexico, he recognized that the drug wars had become a national problem. He used the army against the gangs. Critics, however, had charged that using soldiers against drug gangs was like attacking hornet nests with a baseball bat. The army is not trained to fight criminals, especially criminals who have broken up into innumerable hostile gangs.[3]

The illicit drug industry in Mexico seems to be afflicted with a deadly sort of anarchy, but the cartel leaders themselves appear to be talented organizers in other ways. They have not only subverted Mexican officials, police officers, and soldiers, but they have brought other criminals into their organizations. For its enforcers, the Juárez cartel uses a gang of degenerate murderers called La Linea. Juárez authorities believe La Linea is responsible for an unsolved wave of murders of young women since 1990. The La Linea thugs are noteworthy for sheer, gratuitous cruelty. In one case, they duct-taped a victim's nose and mouth and watched him suffocate. Other victims' bodies have been found with broken bones and other signs of torture. Decapitations have been common. The gangs use their reputation for cruelty to terrorize the population. Last December, they extorted school teachers' Christmas bonus money by threatening to kidnap their pupils.

The cartels recruit gangs on both sides of the border. The Tijuana cartels have long used youths in American street gangs to enforce their policies in both Tijuana and San Diego. An El Paso street gang, the Barrio Aztecas, has been recruited by Juárez's La Linea to help the Mexican gang with enforcement.

The Mexican drug lords have expanded into illegal immigration. Each cartel "owns" a section of the border. To operate in that area, a coyote has to pay a healthy fee. The money for that fee, of course, comes from the illegal immigrants. According to one report, the fee is based on the number and type of immigrants and the time consumed by the trip. For Mexicans (and, presumably, other Latin Americans),

Mexican soldiers escort Oswaldo Munos Gonzalez during his presentation to the press in Ciudad Juárez, Mexico, in September 2009. According to the army, Munos is a member of the La Linea drug gang and is a suspect in connection with 40 murders. *(AP Photo/Heber Chavez)*

$2,000 a week; for "exotics" like Chinese or Middle Easterners, $10,000 a week.[4] The coyote trade, once a mom-and-pop operation, is becoming a cartel sideline. Only the cartels have the money and connections to send professional enforcers to collect from former pollos. They have been collecting for years from associates who "lost" drug shipments— whether they actually embezzled them or had them confiscated by law enforcement. These enforcers, *bajadores,* or "takedown specialists," play several roles on the bloody frontier. They collect payments for the cartels, murder whomever the kingpins would like to see eliminated, and act as freelance bandits, stealing drug shipments and taking over groups of migrants.

THE MOST IMPORTANT LESSON: SUBMISSION

In the July–August 2009 issue of *Mother Jones*, Reporter Charles Bowden tells the story of Emilio Gutierrez Soto, a Mexican newspaper reporter who fled to the United States after the Mexican Army tried to kill him. His crime was reporting a robbery by six soldiers at a rundown boarding house for migrants. He was picked up by an army colonel and taken before a general, who threatened him with death.

Believing that his life was still in danger, Gutierrez filed a complaint with the public safety commissioner and one with the National Commission on Human rights. Then a woman he knew, who was dating a soldier, called him and told him the soldiers were planning to kill him. The soldiers had already killed so many people that Gutierrez didn't hesitate. He got his 15-year-old son (he is a single parent) and drove to the United States.

Gutierrez says the army has taken over northern Mexico. His big mistake was criticizing anyone in authority. He didn't know his place.

Bowden commented in his article, "I remember once being in a small town when the then president of Mexico descended like a god with an entourage and massive security. The poor fled into their shanties until it was over. The streets emptied, and when the president did a staged stroll to greet his subjects, there was no one standing on the sidewalk except party hacks."[5]

Newsweek reported on a man called "Manuel," who was stopped by gun-wielding men in front of his family on a street in Phoenix and forced into a car. He later called his wife and said, "Tell the kids I'm okay," and hung up. His wife told the police. Then she got a phone call from a strange man who said Manuel owed money for drugs and demanded a million dollars and Manuel's Cadillac for ransom. Two men came for the Cadillac, but police stopped them. The men, illegal immigrants, knew only that a man had paid them to take the car and drive it to Tucson.

The police believe that Manuel, who is still missing, was a drug dealer who lost a load. "He was probably brought to Mexico to answer for that," said Lieutenant Lauri Burgett, head of the Phoenix Police Department's home invasion and kidnapping squad.[6] Phoenix has recently become the kidnap capital of the country, entirely because of the Mexican cartels' operations in the United States. And even if Manuel was taken to Mexico, the fact that his car was headed for Tucson indicates that the cartel has a base in the United States.

The cartels, in fact, have many U.S. bases. Their operations are not confined to border states. Police have records of cartel activity as far away as Anchorage, Alaska, and police in Atlanta, Georgia, say their city is "the new southwest border" because of all the Mexican drug activity there. Atlanta, like El Paso, is a regional transportation hub.

Most of the kidnappings occur because of problems in the drug trade, but many also concern human smuggling. Currently, the procedure in human smuggling is for the coyotes to turn their pollos over to *dueños* (chaperones) who run "drop houses" where the "chickens" are kept until they pay their fees. Early in 2009, the Maricopa County Sheriff's Department's Human Smuggling Unit heard from relatives of a would-be immigrant that the man was being held by smugglers who demanded $3,500. The deputies located the drop house in Phoenix, broke through its boarded-up windows and doors, and found several dozen pollos, barefoot and famished. A half-dozen smugglers were arrested, and the officers confiscated two pistols, a shotgun, and a Taser-like device "used against people when they're on the phone, begging their relatives for cash," according to Lieutenant Joe Sousa, the unit commander.[7]

Attorney General Eric Holder has called the activities of the Mexican drug cartels "a national security threat."[8] President Barack Obama sent 500 more federal agents to the border in 2009. The problem will not be solved merely by putting agents on the border. If every single member of the Border Patrol were assigned to the Mexican border 24

Using a camera submerged in a car's gasoline tank, a Border Patrol agent searches for drugs inside a suspicious vehicle at the Falfurrias, Texas, border checkpoint. *(Diego Giudice/Corbis)*

hours a day, with no additional shifts for relief—leaving nobody to monitor televisions and sensors, maintain vehicles, horses, and aircraft, and no supervisors and administrators—there would be a tenth of a mile between each agent. Instead of merely standing guard, however, the new agents and those already on the border will attack several problems.

The new effort to alleviate the Mexican drug problem looks like a new challenge for BORTAC, the Border Patrol unit that helps train foreign drug police, as well as the agency as a whole.

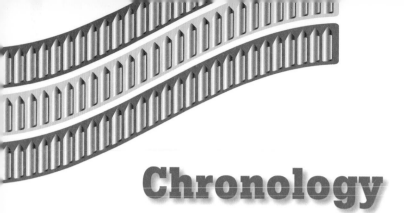

Chronology

1905	Mounted Inspectors (or Watchmen) founded
1906	Brownsville "Mutiny;" racism rampant along the United States–Mexico border
1910	Mexican Revolution begins
1915	Mounted Guards established as an extension of the Watchmen
1916	Villa's raid on Columbus brings revolutionary violence across the border
1917	United States enters World War I
1917	Mexican labor recruited in foreshadowing of Bracero Program
1920	Prohibition begins in the United States, along with smuggling of illegal liquor
1924	Border Patrol established and guns blaze along the border
1929	Mexican Deportation Act; thousands deported
1932	Prohibition ends
1934	Border Patrol Academy founded
1934	Mexican Revolution ends
1941	United States attacked by Japan, enters World War II; manpower shortage in Border Patrol
1942	Bracero Program begins
1954	"Operation Wetback," coupled with more deportations
1965	Bracero Program ends
1976	"Bandit Teams" organized in San Diego to hunt bandits preying on pollos
1979	"Bandit Teams" disbanded

1980	Mariel Boatlift, a flood of criminals and psychiatric patients from Cuba
1983	BORTAC, a tactical unit used in the United States and abroad, founded
1993	Operation Blockade (later Operation Hold the Line) begins in El Paso; later copied in San Diego and Tucson
1998	BORSTAR established to rescue people stranded in the wilderness
1999	"Millennium Bomber" arrested
2000	Elian Gonzales returned to his father amidst a national controversy
2001	9/11 attack; USA PATRIOT Act passed
2002	Homeland Security Act passed
2003	Border Patrol becomes part of Customs and Border Protection, which is part of the Department of Homeland Security
2010	President Barack Obama sends National Guard troops to Mexican border to help Border Patrol

Endnotes

Introduction

1. "Border Patrol History," http://www.cbp.gov/xp/cgov/border_security/border_patrol/border_patrol_ohs/history.xml (Accessed March 18, 2009).
2. Charles Askins, *The Pistol Shooter's Book* (Harrisburg, Pa.: The Telegraph Press, 1957), 113.
3. Erich Krauss, with Alex Pacheco, *On the Line: Inside the U.S. Border Patrol* (New York: Citadel Press, 2004), xx.
4. Ibid., 24.
5. Ibid., xvii–xix.

Chapter 1

1. Joseph Wambaugh, *Lines and Shadows*, (New York: William Morrow, 1984), 32.

Chapter 2

1. WilliamWeir, *The Encyclopedia of African American Military History* (Amherst, N.Y.: Prometheus Books, 2002), 268.
2. Gerald Astor, *The Right to Fight: A History of African Americans in the Military* (Cambridge, Mass.: Da Capo Press, 1988), 80–82.
3. Krauss and Pacheco, 4.
4. Eugene Cunningham, *Triggernometry: A Gallery of Gunfighters* (Caldwell, Idaho: Caxton Printers, Ltd., 1989), 59.
5. Ibid.
6. Jessie Peterson and Thelma Cox Knoles, *Pancho Villa: Intimate Recollections by People Who Knew Him* (New York: Hastings House, 1977), 294.
7. Ibid.
8. Ibid.

Chapter 3

1. Askins, 291–292.
2. Askins, 287.
3. Ibid.
4. Major General Julian S.Hatcher, *Hatcher's Notebook* (Harrisburg, Pa.: Telegraph Press, 1966), 17.
5. Askins, 288.
6. Ibid.
7. Krauss and Pacheco, 18–19.
8. Bill Jordan, *No Second Place Winner* (Concord, N.H.: Police Bookshelf, 2000), 13.
9. Ibid.
10. Ibid.
11. Ibid.
12. Askins, 294–295.
13. Ibid., 315.
14. Ibid., 294–295.

Chapter 4

1. Wendy Koch, "U.S. Urged to Apologize for 1930s Deportations," *U.S.A. Today*, April 5, 2006.

2. Edward Jay Epstein, *Agency of Fear* (New York: G.P. Putnam's Sons, 1977), 31.

3. David F. Musto, M.D., *The American Disease: Origins of Narcotics Control* (New Haven, Conn.: Yale University Press, 1973), 223.

4. Krauss and Pacheco, 25.

5. Ibid., 32.

6. Ibid., 34.

7. Lee Morton II, *The Reaper's Line: Life and Death on the Mexican Border* (Tucson, Ariz.: Nuevo Publishers, 2006), 43.

8. Krauss and Pacheco, 31.

Chapter 5

1. Barry Edmonston and James P. Smith, *The New Americans: Economic, Demographic, and Fiscal Effects of Immigration* (Washington, D.C.: National Academies Press, 1997), 387.

2. Public Institute of California, http://www.ppic.org/content/pubs/cacounts/CC_208KBCC.pdf (Accessed March 18, 2009).

3. Eve Conant and Arian Campo-Flores, "The Enemy Within," *Newsweek*, March 14, 2009; Nathan Thornburgh/Douglas, "The Battle for Arizona," *Time*, June 14, 2010.

4. Arizona Department of Public Safety, "Crime in Arizona 2009," http://azdps.gov/about/Reports/docs/crime_in_arizona_report_2009.pdf (Accessed September 8, 2010).

5. U.S. Department of Justice, "Preliminary Crime Report for 2009," http://www.fbi.gov/ucr/prelimsem2009/index.html (Accessed October 1, 2010).

6. Eduardo Porter, "Illegal Immigrants Are Bolstering Social Security With Billions," *New York Times*, April 5, 2005.

7. Krauss and Pacheco, 112.

8. Brady McCombs, "Cochise Ranch Area Outraged by Killing," *Arizona Daily Star*, http://azstarnet.com/news/local/border/article_32642381-6314-53b4-aff1-570dbd1d6834.html (Accessed July 13, 2010).

9. Deborah Tedford, "Glenn Spencer's American Patrol Group Under Fire by U.S. Military Forces?," SIA News, http://www.sianews.com/modules.php?name=News&file=article&sid=985 (Accessed July 13, 2010).

10. Krauss and Pacheco, 109.

11. Ibid.

12. Susan A. Carter, "U.S. Tipping Mexico to Minuteman Patrols," *DailyBulletin.com*, May 8, 2006, http://www.dailybulletin.com/news/ci_3799653 (Accessed September 8, 2010).

13. Minority Staff of the Committee on Homeland Security, U.S. House of Representatives, *The U.S. Border Patrol: Failure of the Administration to Deliver a Comprehensive Land Border Strategy Leaves our Nation's Borders Vulnerable* (Washington, 2005).

Chapter 6

1. Wambaugh, 10.

2. Ibid., 13.

3. Ibid., 24.

4. Krauss and Pacheco, 49.

5. Ibid., 48.

6. Wambaugh, 32.

7. Krauss and Pacheco, 52.

8. Wambaugh, 111.

9. Krauss and Pacheco, 53.

10. Wambaugh, 266–283.

11. Krauss and Pacheco, 55.
12. Ibid., 56.
13. Ibid., 57.
14. Ibid., 58–59.

Chapter 7
1. Krauss and Pacheco, 99.
2. Ibid., 101.
3. Ibid., 102.
4. Ibid., 103-104.
5. Ibid., 128.
6. Ibid., 130.
7. Ibid., 137.

Chapter 8
1. "U.S. Expanding 'Virtual Fence' on Canadian Border," FoxNews.com, April 1, 2009, http://www.foxnews.com/story/0,2933,511925,00.html (Accessed April 25, 2009).
2. CTV News, "U.S. Security Boss Clarifies Comments About Border," http://www.ctv.ca/servlet/ArticleNews/story/ CTVNews/20090421/USA_Border _090421/20090421 (Accessed July 13, 2010).

Chapter 9
1. Krauss and Pacheco, xvi–xvii.
2. Officer Down Memorial Page, "U.S. Border Patrol," http://www.odmp.org/agency/4830 -united-states-department-of-homeland-security---customs-and-border-protection---border-patrol-u.s.-government (Accessed September 8, 2010).
3. Conant and Campo-Flores, "The Enemy Within."
4. Ibid.
5. Charles Bowden, "We Bring Fear," *Mother Jones*, July–August 2009.
6. Conant and Campo-Flores, The Enemy Within."
7. Tim Padgett, "On the Bloody Border," *Time*, May 4, 2009.
8. Ibid.

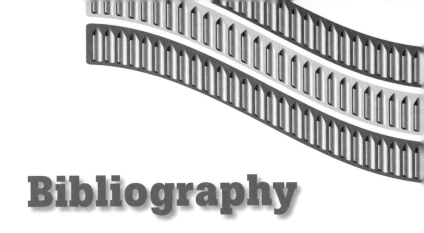

Bibliography

Books and Periodicals

Askins, Charles. *The Pistol Shooter's Book.* Harrisburg, Pa.: Stackpole Company, 1957.

Astor, Gerald. *The Right to Fight: A History of African Americans in the Military.* Cambridge, Mass.: Da Capo Press, 1988.

Bowden, Charles. "We Bring Fear." *Mother Jones,* July–August, 2009.

Conant, Eve, and Arian Campo-Flores. "The Enemy Within." *Newsweek,* April 22, 2009.

Cunningham, Eugene. *Triggernometry: A Gallery of Gunfighters.* Caldwell, Idaho: Caxton Printers, Ltd., 1989.

Edmonston, Barry, and James P. Smith. *The New Americans.* Washington, D.C.: National Academies Press, 1977.

Epstein, Edward J. *Agency of Fear.* New York: G.P. Putnam's Sons, 1977.

Jordan, Bill. *No Second Place Winner.* Concord, N. H.: Police Bookshelf, 2000.

Krauss, Erich, with Alex Pacheco. *On the Line: Inside the U.S. Border Patrol.* New York: Citadel Press, 2004.

Mason, Herbert Molloy Jr. *The Great Pursuit.* New York: Random House, 1970.

Metz, Leon Claire. *The Shooters.* New York: Berkley Books, 1996.

Minority Staff of the Committee on Homeland Security, U.S. House of Representatives. *The U.S. Border Patrol: Failure of the Administration to Deliver a Comprehensive Land Border Strategy Leaves Our Nation's Borders Vulnerable.* Washington, D.C., 2005.

Morton, Lee II. *The Reaper's Line: Life and Death on the Mexican Border.* Tucson, Ariz.: Nuevo Publishers, 2000.

Musto, David F., M.D. *The American Disease: Origins of Narcotics Control.* New Haven, Conn.: Yale University Press, 1973.

Padgett, Tim. "On the Bloody Border." *Time,* May 4, 2010.

Peterson, Jessie, and Thelma Cox Knoles. *Pancho Villa: Intimate Recollections by People Who Knew Him.* New York: Hastings House, 1977.

Wambaugh, Joseph. *Lines and Shadows.* New York: William Morrow, 1984.

Weir, William. *The Encyclopedia of African American Military History.* Amherst, N.Y.: Prometheus Books, 2002.

Web Sites

Fox News. "U.S. Expanding Virtual Fence on Canadian Border." Available online. URL: http://www.foxnews.com/story/0,2933,511925,00.html. Accessed April 25, 2009.

Sara A. Carter. "U.S. Tipping Mexico to Minuteman Patrols," *Daily Bulletin*. Available online. URL: http://www.dailybulletin.com/news/ci_3799653. Accessed March 17, 2009.

Public Institute of California. "Crime, Corrections, and California." Available online. URL: http://www.ppic.org/content/pubs/cacounts/CC_208KBCC.pdf. Accessed March 18, 2009.

Further Resources

Print

Ezell, Edward C. *Handguns of the World*. New York: Barnes & Noble, 1981. Contains information on the Pershing expedition to capture Pancho Villa.

Hartink, A.E. *The Complete Encyclopedia of Pistols and Revolvers*. Lisse, Netherlands: Rebo Publishers, 2008. Provides information on the various guns used by the Border Patrol, including the latest, the Heckler & Koch P2000.

Hatcher, Major Gen. Julian S. *Hatcher's Notebook*. Harrisburg, Pa.: Stackpole, 1966. General Hatcher investigated the report that the machine guns at Columbus were useless because they jammed during Villa's raid. He found that the reports were untrue.

Hatcher, Major General Julian S. *Textbook of Pistols and Revolvers*. Plantersville, S.C.: Small-Arms Technical Publishing Company, 1935. A comprehensive resource for those interested in learning about pistols and revolvers.

Smith, W.H.B., and Joseph Smith. *Small Arms of the World*. Harrisburg, Pa.: Stackpole Company, 1960. Resource covering handheld guns.

As the greatest threat (other than acts of war) from beyond U.S. borders seems to be from drug traffickers, the following books help the reader to understand the drug-smuggling problem, which has been going on for a long time:

Baum, Dan. *Smoke and Mirrors: The War on Drugs and the Politics of Failure*. New York: Back Bay Books, 1997. A critical look at the so-called War on Drugs.

Cockburn, Leslie. *Out of Control: The Story of the Reagan Administration's Secret War in Nicaragua, the Illegal Arms Pipeline, and the Contra Drug Connection*. New York: Grove/Atlantic, Inc., 1987. Details CIA involvement in the drug trade in Latin America.

McCoy, Alfred W. *The Politics of Heroin: CIA Complicity in the Global Drug Trade*. Revised ed. Brooklyn, N.Y.: Lawrence Hill Books, 2003. Looks at the drug trade in Southeast Asia, Australia, and Europe.

Scott, Peter Dale, and Jonathan Marshall. *Cocaine Politics: Drugs, Armies, and the CIA in Central America*. Updated ed. Berkeley, Calif.: University of California Press, 1998. Another look at drugs and Contras.

Weir, William. *In the Shadow of the Dope Fiend: America's War on Drugs.* North Haven, Conn.: Archon Press, 1997. The history of U.S. involvement with drugs.

Following are books concerned with aspects of the Old West:

Horan, James D. *Desperate Men.* New York: G.P. Putnam's Sons, 1949. The history of the James gang and Butch Cassidy's Wild Bunch.
Horan, James D. *The Gunfighters.* New York: Crown Publishers, 2003. Covers Billy the Kid and other Western gunmen.
Rosa, Joseph G. *The Gunfighter, Man or Myth?* Norman, Okla.: University of Oklahoma Press, 1969. Examines stories about Western gunfighters.
Weir, William. *Written with Lead.* New York: Cooper Square Press, 2003. American gunfights from the Revolution to the D.C. snipers.
Weir, William. *History's Greatest Lies.* Beverly, Mass.: Fair Winds Press, 2009. Provides information on the Wyatt Earp legend.

Online

National Border Patrol Museum
http://www.borderpatrolmuseum.com
The National Border Patrol Museum's official Web site.

The New York Times: Topics: Border Patrol, U.S.
http://topics.nytimes.com/top/reference/timestopics/organizations/b/border_patrol_us/index.html
Border Patrol articles in the New York Times.

USBorderPatrol.com
http://www.usborderpatrol.com/Border_Patrol90html
An overview of the Border Patrol.

U.S. Customs and Border Protection
http://www.cbp.gov/
Official Web site of U.S. Customs and Border Protection.

U.S. Department of Homeland Security Web Site
http://www.dhs.gov/
A useful source of information on border security and immigration.

Index

119

About the Author

William Weir was a military police private first class and a U.S. army combat correspondent and photographer during the Korean War. After leaving the army, he became a newspaper reporter and photographer, then a public relations specialist for a telephone company. While working for the phone company, he wrote freelance magazine articles on a variety of subjects, but specialized in crime. He has written 12 previous books, most of them on military history.